Michael Halliday

Windows 10
For Seniors

1st Edition

Notice of Liability

The publisher and the author make no representations or warranties with respect to the accuracy or completeness of the contents of this book and specifically disclaim all warranties, including without limitation warranties or fitness for a particular purpose.

No warranty may be created or extended by sales or promotional materials. The advice and strategies contained herein may not be suitable for every situation. Accordingly, this work is sold with the understanding that the publisher is not engaged in rendering legak, accounting or other professional services. If professional assistane ia required, the services of a competent professional person should be sought. Neither the publisher nor the author shall be liable dor damages arising herefrom.

The fact that an organisation or website is referred to in this work as a citation and/or a potential source of further information does not mean that the publisher or the author endorses the information the organisation or website may provide or recommendations that it may make.

Furthermore, readers should be awar that internet websites listed in this work may have changed or disappeared between when this work was first published and when it is read.

Trademarks

All trademarks are acknowledged as belonging to their respective companies.

Table of Contents

Chapter One - Getting Acquainted With Windows 10

Chapter Two - Finding Your Way in Windows 10

Chapter Three - Fundamentals of Windows 10

Chapter Four - Working With Files and Folders

Chapter Five - Applications That Come With Windows

Chapter Six - Customise the Way Windows Looks and Acts

Chapter Seven - Managing Your Hardware

Chapter Eight - The Internet

Chapter Nine - Setting Up and Using Email

Chapter Ten - Working With Multimedia

Chapter Eleven - Keep Your Computer and Data Secure

Chapter Twelve - Troubleshooting & Maintenance

Index

CHAPTER 1

Getting Acquainted With Windows 10

In Chapter One, we see how to get started with Windows 10. We take a look at the main elements of the interface such as the Desktop, Start Menu and Taskbar.

We also examine some new features that include Virtual desktops, the Action Centre, Task Switcher and the new personal assistant, Cortana. Learning how to work with tiles and groups is covered as well.

Meet Windows 10

Windows 10 is Microsoft's replacement for the unlamented and almost universally unpopular Windows 8. One of the main design aims with this operating system has been to bridge the gap between computers and mobile devices without alienating users of either.

A feature that clearly demonstrates this is the way that a two-in-one device, such as Microsoft's Surface Pro, automatically switches between computer mode and tablet mode whenever a keyboard is attached or unattached.

The newer operating system corrects the mistakes made in Windows 8 by taking the best parts of previous Windows editions and combining them with some new features to create a cohesive package that is a considerable improvement in nearly every respect.

Another plus is that the upgrade process is straightforward and, providing they are prepared to wait for it, is free for most non-corporate users of older Windows editions.

The introduction of Windows 10 also confirms the direction that Microsoft is taking with Windows. It has brought to an end the grand and dramatic changes seen in previous editions and has replaced them with small and more subtle tweaks similar to those seen on Android and iOS devices. Expect to see this trend continue in the future.

Windows 10 is the dual-purpose operating system that Microsoft intended Windows 8 to be but wasn't. Furthermore, it provides the groundwork for future Windows editions that will be able to run effortlessly on whatever type of device the manufacturers can dream up. It won't just be dual-purpose but triple-purpose and more.

This comes later though. What Microsoft is offering right now with Windows 10 is a fast, well featured and functional operating system that is equally at home on a tablet or smartphone as it is on a desktop computer. Apple have been doing it for years with iOS; Microsoft have now caught up.

If you're still running Windows 7 or Windows 8, you've got absolutely nothing lose and quite a bit to gain by making the jump to Windows 10. If you're still on Windows XP, well, you've probably got your reasons!

Windows 8 and Windows 10 have been the initial steps in a transition from operating system to ecosystem. This is Microsoft's second attempt at bringing us the future, and while it is still not perfect, this time it's a lot closer to reality.

Configuring the Lock Screen

When you switch your computer on and start Windows 10 for the first time, you are taken to the Lock screen. The main purpose of this screen is to provide a security barrier that prevents malware such as login scripts from taking control of your computer.

The Lock screen also has a secondary function – it can be configured to display information of various types. For example: reminders of appointments, tell you when you have new email messages, display weather alerts, etc.

Configuring the Lock Screen
You can configure the Lock screen to display detailed information from one app and basic details from up to seven other apps.

To do it:

1. Click anywhere on the Lock screen or tap any key. This takes you to the Desktop (via the Sign-in screen - see page 11)

2. Right-click on the Desktop and select **Personalize** from the menu

3. The Personalization Settings screen opens – select **Lock screen** at the left

cont'd

4. Click the icon under **Choose an app to show detailed status**

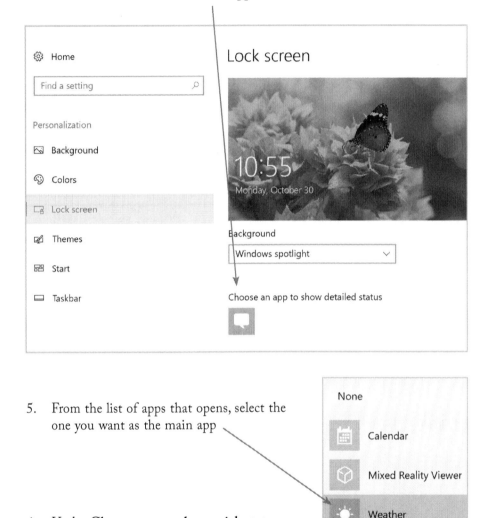

5. From the list of apps that opens, select the one you want as the main app

6. Under **Choose apps to show quick status,** click each icon in turn and choose an app from the list that opens

7. Close the Personalization window by clicking the **X** button at the top-right. Your settings will now be applied to the Lock screen

Log-on to Windows

Click anywhere on the Lock screen to access the Sign-in screen. It will open as shown below:

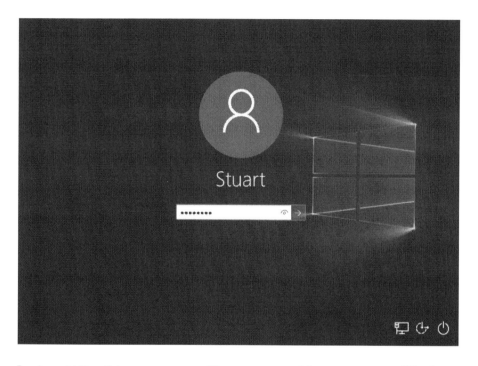

In the middle of the screen, you will see a password box – enter your Windows password and tap **Enter** on the keyboard. Assuming the password is correct, you will now be taken to the Desktop, which we look at on the next page.

At the bottom-right of the Sign-in screen you will notice three buttons. From left to right, the purpose of these are:

- Configure your Internet settings (assuming you are not already connected)

- Access a list of accessibility options, such as an on-screen keyboard and sticky keys. Some of the options here may be of particular interest to senior citizens!

- Shut the computer down

Above the password box, there is a large circle. This is a placeholder for your account picture, if and when you add one. We explain how to do this on page 92.

And thats about it for the Sign-in screen. The next thing you will see is the Desktop.

The Desktop

After signing in, you are taken to the Desktop. Initially, it is empty apart from the Recycle Bin at the top-left. Running along the bottom of the Desktop is the Taskbar, which we look at on the next page.

The purpose of the Desktop is to provide an easily accessible location where you can put shortcuts to programs and features you use often. When you open programs or folders, they appear on the Desktop. You can also create folders on the Desktop and use them to categorise and organise your files and programs. To do this, right-click an empty part of the Desktop, and go to **New > Folder**.

On the Desktop, files, folders and programs are represented by icons – double-clicking on an icon will open the item. To place a shortcut to a favourite item on the Desktop, locate the item and then right-click on it. Click **Send to**, and then click **Desktop (create shortcut)**. The shortcut icon appears on your Desktop.

To move an item to the Desktop, browse to where it is located, left-click on it and then just drag it to the Desktop and release it. The position of icons on the Desktop can be arranged in the same way – left-click and drag.

Groups of icons can be selected by left-clicking on the screen and dragging to create a box around them. You can then drag the icons as a group or delete them. Right-clicking on the screen offers a number of other icon-related options as well. These include re-sizing and sorting by various criteria.

To remove an item from the Desktop, right-click on it and then click **Delete**. Note that if the item is a shortcut, only the shortcut is removed; the original item, wherever it is, is not deleted.

The Taskbar and its Functions

The Taskbar is the long horizontal bar at the bottom of your screen. Unlike the Desktop, which can get obscured by open windows, the Taskbar is almost always visible. It has four main sections:

- The Start button at the far-left, which opens the Start menu

- The search box, which enables you to find anything on the computer

- A middle section, which shows you the programs and files you have open, and allows you to quickly switch between them

- The Notification area at the right, which includes a clock and various icons that indicate the status of certain programs and computer settings

Notification Area

The icons on the Notification area indicate the status of open items or provide access to settings. When you hold the mouse over a particular icon, you will see that icon's name or the status of a setting.

For example, the network icon tells you whether or not you are connected to the Internet. The icons displayed on the Notification area depend on the programs and services on the computer and how it was set up.

Double-clicking an icon usually opens the program or setting associated with it. Occasionally, an icon will display a small pop-up window to notify you about something, such as the successful installation of a new hardware device.

Middle Section

The middle section of the Taskbar enables you to keep track of what's happening on your computer. If you have several windows open at the same time, they will often cover each other making it difficult to see what items are underneath, or remember what's open.

The Taskbar solves this by showing an icon for each program. So if you have three folders open for example, holding the mouse over the folder icon on the

Taskbar will reveal thumbnails of all the folders with the names of each one clearly displayed. The contents of each folder can be displayed and they can be closed from their thumbnail. You can also right-click on the folder icon in the Taskbar and close all the folders simultaneously.

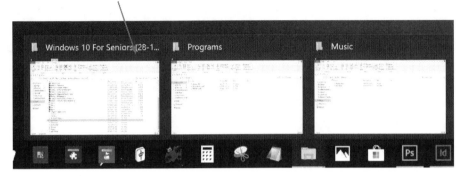

Furthermore, the Taskbar displays different icons for different types of item. Have a Notepad note open as well as the folders, and on the Taskbar you'll see both a folder icon and a Notepad icon.

This part of the Taskbar also has four default buttons. The Task view button opens thumbnails of all running programs; the Microsoft Edge button opens the Edge Internet browser; the File Explorer button lets you explore your computer; and the Store button takes you to the Windows Store.

Moving left along the Taskbar we have the search box. This lets you search not only the computer but the Internet as well. When you use it for the first time, Windows 10's personal assistant, Cortana, will spring to life. We take a look at Cortana on pages 22-23. If you don't want a search box on the Taskbar, you can get rid of it by right-clicking on the search box and going to **Cortana** and then clicking **Hidden**.

Other options are available from this right-click menu as well. For example, clicking **Taskbar settings** at the bottom of it opens a range of Taskbar options. You can lock it in its current location, move it to the top or either side of the Desktop, make the Taskbar buttons and icons smaller, and even auto-hide it so that it is only visible when you mouse over it.

You will also see options for the Notification area. Here, you will be able to choose which icons to display, deactivate system icons, disable app notifications and specify which apps can show notifications.

At the far-left of the Taskbar is the Start menu button. This has one purpose – open the Start menu as we see on the next page.

Working With the Start Menu

The Start menu is the main gateway to your computer's programs, folders and settings. It's called a menu because it provides a list of choices, just as a restaurant menu does. And as 'start' implies, it's often the place that you'll go to start or open things. For example:

- Start programs

- Access commonly used system folders

- Search for files, folders and programs

- Access and adjust your computer's settings

- Turn the computer off

- Log off from Windows or switch to a different user account

To open the Start menu, click the **Start menu** button at the left of the Taskbar or tap the **Windows key** on your keyboard. It will open as shown below:

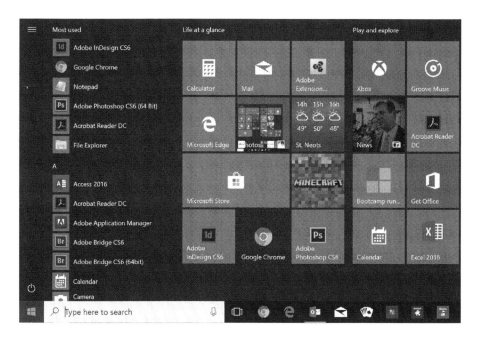

Start Menu Layout

At the bottom-left, third icon up, you'll see a button that lets you access your account. Click on the button to open the settings for the account, to switch to the Lock screen and to sign out from Windows. Also, if you at some point create more user accounts, you will be able to switch between them from here.

cont'd

Below the account button is Settings - this lets you configure just about every aspect of Windows.

Below Settings is Power. This gives you three options - Sleep, Shutdown and Restart.

At the top-right of the Start menu are two sets of apps. At the left is **Life at a glance** – a collection of productivity apps that you will mainly use for work and, at the right, **Play and explore** – a collection of apps that will mainly be used to keep yourself entertained. Both collections are comprised of 'live tiles' that can show updated content.

The Windows 10 Start menu is also quite customisable (we look at how to do this on page 93). For example, you can change the background colour, re-arrange the position of the various tiles and pin your favourite apps on it. More importantly, you can specify which system items appear on the menu – Control Panel, Documents, This PC, etc.

Organising the Start Menu With Tiles

Tile collections are known as groups and it is easy to create your own. This can be very useful with regard to organising the Start menu. Do it as follows:

1. Locate the first tile to be placed in your new group and drag it to an empty part of the Start menu. As you do so, you'll notice a blue bar appear; when it has, release the tile. (If you release the tile before the blue bar appears, it will be added to an existing group.)

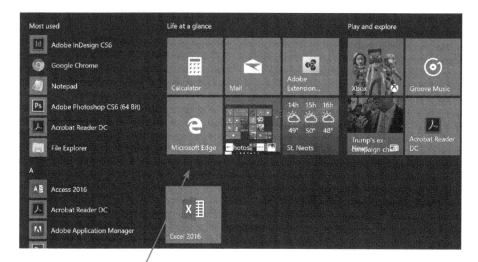

2. There will be a gap between the new tile and the one above it. Move your mouse to the gap and a **Name group** link will appear. Click to open it and then type in a name for your group.

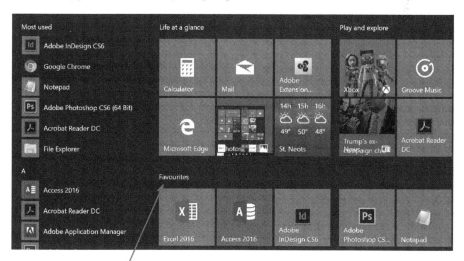

In the example above, we have created a new tile group called Favourites.

Virtual Desktops and How to Use Them

What is a Virtual Desktop?

If you have a single monitor attached to your computer, you have one screen, i.e. desktop – on which to run all your apps and programs. This is fine for light use, such as having a couple of programs open at the same time. For heavy use though, where you have lots of programs running concurrently, things can quickly get confusing or just plain cumbersome.

This is where virtual desktops come into play. Effectively, they are extra desktops and you can have as many as you need. This enables you to create different workspaces or screens for different applications. For example, you can have your real desktop populated with work apps and a virtual desktop populated with leisure related apps.

Creating a Virtual Desktop

Go to the Taskbar and click the **Task View** button (alternatively, press the Windows and Tab keys simultaneously). Doing so reveals all the virtual desktops that have been set up. Initially, there won't be any and all you'll see is a **New desktop** button at the far-right.

Click the **New desktop** button and a virtual desktop is created. Click it again to create a second one, and so on as we see below where four have been created:

Desktop 1 is the real desktop – the others are all virtual. You will notice that while they look identical to the real desktop, they won't have any programs running on them.

Click on any one of the desktops, real or virtual, to go to it. You can switch to any of the others at any time simply by clicking the **Task View** button, which will reveal them all as shown above.

If you have programs or windows open on a virtual desktop, they are displayed on the thumbnail image of that desktop on the Task View interface. This is demonstrated in the screenshot at the top of the next page, where you will see that virtual desktop 2 has been selected (indicated by the blue border).

cont'd

When you move your mouse over a desktop that has programs open on it, each of the programs is displayed as a large thumbnail. Click on one of the thumbnails to make that program (and the corresponding desktop) active.

You can move programs among the different desktops you've set up. To do so, click the **Task View** button to reveal all the desktops, hover the mouse over the desktop containing the program to be moved, click the program's thumbnail and simply drag it to the required desktop.

Another way is to right-click on the program's thumbnail, select **Move to** and then the required desktop.

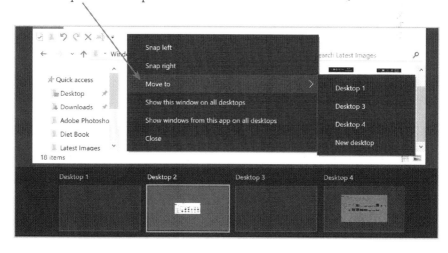

To close a desktop, click the **Task View** button on the Taskbar to bring up the Task View interface. Move your mouse over the thumbnail for the desktop you want to close. Click the **X** button in the upper-right corner of the thumbnail.

Stay Updated With the Action Centre

Windows has long had a feature called Notifications that opens an advisory pop-up window on the screen whenever something has happened that it thinks the user should be aware of. A typical example is when a program has automatically updated itself. The problem with this is that these notifications are easily overlooked, particularly if you are busy with something else. The Action Centre in Windows 10 offers the solution. Basically, it provides a way of reviewing your notification history so you can check something you neglected to look at earlier, or indeed if there is anything you have missed completely.

To access the Action Centre, click the ▣ button at the far-right of the Taskbar. You can also open it by pressing the **Windows key + A.**

Notifications are categorised and displayed by type, e.g. Autoplay, Security and Maintenance, etc. Click a notification to open it and activate any actions that need to be carried out. At the right of many notifications, you'll see a down-arrow – click this to reveal more details. Hover the mouse over the notification to reveal an **X** button – click this to remove the notification from the panel.

At the bottom of the Action Centre are 'quick action' buttons that provide access to commonly used features. Examples of this are **Tablet mode**, which switches Windows 10 between Desktop and Tablet modes; and **All settings**, which provides access to all the computer's settings.

VPN lets you quickly connect or disconnect from a virtual private network; **Note** lets you quickly create a note in OneNote; **Location** turns your computer's location-based services on or off; and **Quiet hours** mutes all the notifications. If you click the **All settings** button and go to **System > Notifications and actions**, you will see a number of customisation options for the Action Centre. For example: specify which 'quick actions' to show, turn app notifications off and set notifications to show on the Lock screen.

Work Efficiently With the Task Switcher

Windows 10 gives you several ways to switch between open windows and programs – collectively known as 'tasks'. Being able to do this is essential if you want to work efficiently.

A very useful feature in Windows 10 with regard to this is the way open tasks are highlighted on the Taskbar as we see here at the right.

This provides an at-a-glance view of current tasks and gives you a good idea of what's going on, particularly if you recognize the programs from their icons.

One way of switching between them is the **Alt + Tab keyboard** shortcut, which is known as the Windows Task Switcher. Press the two keys simultaneously to open the Task Switcher and you will see large thumbnails of all the open programs as shown below:

Then, while holding **Alt** down, tap the **Tab** key to flick through the tasks. When you get to the one you want to switch to, release the Alt key – it will then open on the desktop. You will notice that each program has a large text label at the top, which further helps to identify the programs.

It is also possible to close programs from the Task Switcher. Hover the mouse over the program you want to close and an **X** will appear at the top-right corner – click it to close the program.

The Task View button at the immediate right of the Taskbar search box does the same thing – it shows thumbnails of all open programs and allows you to switch between them using the mouse rather than the Tab key.

Meet Cortana - Your Personal Assistant

What is Cortana?

Cortana is Microsoft's version of Apple's 'Siri' and Google's 'Google Now' personal assistants. It will help you find things on your computer, manage your calendar, find files and even chat with you. Furthermore, Cortana learns as it goes along, so the more you use it the more personalised your experience with it becomes.

There are two ways to interact with Cortana: by text entry on your keyboard and by voice via a microphone. Your computer may have one built-in but, if not, stand microphones are available very cheaply and headsets with microphones are available for just a little more.

Configuring a Microphone

If you want to operate Cortana by voice, you must first set up the microphone.

1. Click the **Start button** at the left of the Taskbar and then click **Settings >** **Time & Language**

2. Click **Speech** on the left

3. In the Microphone section, click the **Get started** button

4. In the **Set up your mic** window, click **Next**

5. You will be given a sentence to read aloud. If the microphone picks up your voice the setup is done. Click the **Finish** button

Setting Up Cortana

Before you can use Cortana, it needs some basic configuration. Get started by clicking in the search box to the right of the Start button.

A window will pop up offering a brief overview of what Cortana can do for you. If you are not interested in using the feature, click the **Not interested** button – this lets you stick with the standard Windows search utility. If you do want to use Cortana, however, click the **Next** button.

You'll then need to agree to a privacy statement since, in order to work, Cortana needs information about you. This includes your computer's location, your contacts, web history and so on.

Cortana only works with a Microsoft account, as it saves information about you online. So if you're currently using a local Windows account to log in to your computer, you'll be prompted to switch to a Microsoft account or, if you haven't got one, to create one - see page 159

Personalising Cortana

Cortana will build up a profile about you as you use it and you can speed up this process by telling it what you're interested in. Click in the search box and click the **Notebook** icon.

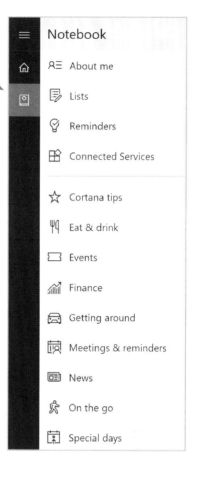

All the information Cortana holds on you is kept in the Notebook. Right at the top of the Notebook is an **About me** link. Click this to edit your name (how Cortana addresses you) and your locations – home, work, etc. Cortana will then be able to give travel directions, traffic updates before you travel and so on.

At the bottom-left is a **Settings** button. This lets you configure Cortana in a number of ways. These include enabling 'Hey Cortana', which lets you make a voice query simply by saying Hey Cortana rather than clicking the microphone icon each time

You can also use the Notebook to tell Cortana what your interests are. This is done by opening the various categories and seeing what options are available; these will be different for each category.

The Sports category, for example, lets you specify teams you want to follow and be updated on upcoming matches and scores as they come in.

Using Cortana

Once it has been set up, you can query Cortana by text (click in the search box) or by voice (click the microphone button at the right of the search box). Whichever method you use, Cortana will then display a summary of information it thinks you'll be interested in. You'll get this every time you click in the box but, over time as the feature gets to know your interests, these will become more relevant.

Cortana can search your PC for specific files, applications and settings. You can ask it more general questions, and even use it to search the web – just ask it a question as you would a person. You can also give Cortana commands such as sending an email or making an appointment for a certain date.

User Accounts and Their Applications

Windows 10 makes it possible for any number of people to use a computer by allowing each person to have their own personal account. Depending on the type of account, they can configure and personalise them by changing the wallpaper and colours, they can install software that's only accessible from their account, and install and set up hardware.

Being able to do this is particularly useful in a home environment where several family members all use the computer. By giving each their own account, which they can customise to suit their specific requirements and tastes, a single computer can be used sensibly and without conflict.

Another useful application of user accounts is to password-protect the main administrator account and then create standard accounts for the kids. They can use the computer but won't be able to compromise its security or performance due to the limitations placed on standard accounts.

Account Types
When Windows 10 is installed, an administrator account is created by default. However, the user also has the option of creating and using a standard account. Lets take a look at both types and see the pros and cons:

- **Administrator Accounts** – the administrator account has complete access to the computer and can make any desired changes. Most people use it simply because it's already there – it's the default account. The drawback is that any program that is run on an administrator account also has complete access to the computer – this is how malware and viruses get on to a user's system

  Administrator accounts come in two types: a Microsoft account, to which you have to sign in with a Microsoft registered email address and password; and a local account, which just requires a user name and password. The drawback with the latter is that you won't be able to download apps from the Windows Store (although you can browse it) and some Microsoft apps on the computer won't work

- **Standard Accounts** – standard accounts are much safer as they do not allow users to make unauthorised changes that affect the system. If a standard account user tries to install a program for example, they will need to enter a password, i.e. they need permission, before being allowed to.

  However, while they may not be able to install programs, make changes to global settings, etc, they will be able to do just about anything else. Therefore, on a day-to-day basis, being restricted to a standard account will present no problems to the average user.

Creating a New User

Creating an account for another person to use is very easy to do:

1. Click the **Start** button and then click **Settings**

2. Click **Accounts**

3. Click **Family & other people**

4. If the account is for a member of the family, click **Add a family member**

5. Select either **Add a child** or **Add an adult** (the first option sets restrictions on what the child can do on the computer)

6. Enter the new user's email address and click **Next**

7. In the **Add this person?** window, click the **Confirm** button

8. The next window tells you that an invitation has been sent to the user's email address and that they'll need to accept the invitation in order to change settings for their new account. Click **Close.** A standard account is now available for the new user to log in to

Signing in to, or Switching, Accounts

Once a new account has been created, when the computer is started, a login option for the new user will be available on the login screen. Click in it, enter the password and the account will open.

It is also possible to switch to a different account without having to turn the computer off and then back on. To do this, click the Start button to open the Start menu. At the lower left of the menu, click the account currently being used to reveal a list of all the accounts on the PC. Click the desired account to open the login screen where the account's password will need to be entered.

Changing Account Type

You may, at some point, wish to change an administrator account to a standard account, or vice versa. This is done in Account settings:

1. Click the **Start** button and go to **Settings, Accounts, Family & other people**

2. Click the required account and then click **Change account type**

3. Select **Administrator** or **Standard User** and click **OK**

Close Windows the Correct Way

When you've had enough of your computer for one day, it's time to close it down. Like many procedures in Windows, there is a right way and a wrong way to do this.

The wrong way is to hit the power button on the computer. Doing this while Windows is running can be the cause of all sorts of problems that include loss of data and possibly even a totally screwed-up Windows installation.

The right way is to click the Start menu button at the left of the Taskbar and then click Power. This will open a menu with three options:

- **Sleep** – Sleep is a power-saving mode that allows your computer to quickly resume full-power operation (typically within several seconds) when you want to start working again. Putting your computer into Sleep mode is like pausing a DVD player—the computer immediately stops what it's doing and is ready to start again when you want to resume working. Use the Sleep Mode option when you're going to be away from your PC for a short while – when you're taking a coffee break, for example

- **Shut down** – clicking Shut down turns off both the computer and Windows completely. This is the option to use when you are not going to be using it for a while

- **Restart** – this is not an option that you will use often. Usually, Restart is used when you want to turn Windows off and back on again. This is often done as a means of resolving spurious problems that can occur with Windows from time to time

Related options can be accessed by clicking your account button on the Start menu. Two of these are:

- **Lock** – clicking Lock takes you to the Lock screen. To get back into Windows it will be necessary to enter the correct password. This can be useful if you need to leave the computer in a secure state for a while

- **Sign out** – this option will sign you out of your account. Note that all running programs will be closed so make sure you save everything first

Keyboard Shortcuts

Windows 10 offers a number of keyboard shortcuts to help with using its various features, such as virtual desktops and the Cortana personal assistant.

Window Snapping

Window snapping (see pages 47-48) helps the user to arrange open windows on the desktop:

- **Windows key + left arrow** – snap active window to the left of the screen

- **Windows key + right arrow** – snap active window to the right of the screen

- **Windows key + up arrow** – snap active window to the top of the screen

- **Windows key + down arrow** – snap active window to the screen bottom

Virtual Desktops

The Windows key can also be used with the virtual desktops feature:

- **Windows key + Ctrl + D** – create a new virtual desktop

- **Windows key + Ctrl + left arrow** – scroll left through your desktops

- **Windows key + Ctrl + right arrow** – scroll right through your desktops

- **Windows key + Ctrl + F4** – close the current desktop

- **Windows key + Tab** – open the task view that shows all open desktops

Cortana

Keyboard shortcuts for Windows 10's personal assistant include:

- **Windows key + Q** – opens Cortana ready for voice input

- **Windows key + S** – opens Cortana ready for typed input

Navigation

Windows 10 keyboard shortcuts apart, there are plenty of old classics that have survived successive versions of the operating system and are still going strong:

- **Windows key + ,** – temporarily hide apps to briefly show the desktop

- **Windows key + D** – minimize apps to go straight to the desktop

- **Windows key + Home** – minimize all windows except the one being used

- **Windows key + L** – lock your PC and go to the Lock screen

- **Windows key + E** – launch File Explorer (aka Windows Explorer)

cont'd

- **Windows key + any number key** – opens the app pinned to the Taskbar in the numbered position, e.g. Win + 2 opens the second app on the Taskbar

- **Windows key + T** – cycle through taskbar items (hit Enter to launch)

- **Windows key + R** – opens the Run dialog box

- **Windows key + U** – cycle through taskbar items (hit Enter to launch)

- **Windows key + Space** – switches input language and keyboard

- **Alt + Up arrow** – go up one level in File Explorer

- **Alt + Left arrow** – go to the previous folder in File Explorer

- **Alt + Right arrow** – go to the next folder in File Explorer

- **Alt + Tab** – switch between windows

- **Alt + F4** – close the current window

- **Alt + Right arrow** – go to the next folder in File Explorer

Pictures, Video and Display
Windows 10 is a very visual OS and there are keyboard shortcuts to help you capture screenshots, record on-screen activity and zoom in and out:

- **Windows key + Print Screen** – takes a screenshot and saves it in the Pictures folder

- **Windows key + G** – opens the Game DVR recorder (if supported by your graphics card).

- **Windows key + Alt + G** – start recording activity in the current window

- **Windows key + P** – switches between display modes (with a secondary display connected)

- **Windows key + Plus** – zoom in using the Magnifier utility

- **Windows key + Minus** – zoom out using the Magnifier utility

CHAPTER 2

Finding Your Way In Windows 10

In Chapter 2, we see how to get around in Windows 10 using a feature known as File Explorer. This is an important part of Windows and, like many parts of the operating system, it's been given a noticeable overhaul in Windows 10.

While the basic layout and functionality of File Explorer will be familiar to anyone who has used Windows XP or later, the Windows 10 version includes a number of new features. We explain how File Explorer works and how it can be used to find and access the various parts of your computer.

We also take a brief look at some important system folders such as This PC and the Control Panel.

Access Your Data With File Explorer

File Explorer (known as Windows Explorer in previous editions of Windows) is a file manager application that provides a graphical interface for accessing your computer's file system. The three main ways to access it are:

1. In the Taskbar search box, type **File** and then tap **Enter** on your keyboard

2. If you're on the Desktop, click the File Explorer icon on the Taskbar

3. Press the **Windows** key and the **E** key simultaneously

File Explorer will open as shown below:

The basic purpose of File Explorer is to provide access to the contents of a given folder. This enables you to work with those contents, whatever they may be. For example, you may want to rename a file, copy it to a different part of the computer or delete it.

File Explorer is designed to help you carry out these actions as easily as possible. Take a look at the address bar – you'll see that it is showing the name of the folder currently being displayed – in this example it is **Quick Access**. This is the folder that File Explorer opens by default and, as the name suggests, it provides access to the folders you use the most. We take a closer look at the Quick Access folder on page 35.

Four folders that will always be present in it are Music, Videos, Documents, and Pictures. These are libraries and we explain their purpose on page 34.

Locating Files and Folders

Due to the hierarchical nature of Windows, you will usually have to navigate through a number of folders and subfolders to find the file you want.

Two ways you can do this are:

1. Open File Explorer and take a look at the navigation pane on the left – if you see the folder that contains the required file, all you have to do is click on it. Its contents will appear in the main File Explorer window

2. If the folder you're after is in the main File Explorer area, double-click it to open it

However, it's more likely that you won't see the required folder in either of these locations. The reason for this is that files, and the folders that contain them, are almost always in subfolders. To illustrate this, consider the Photos folder on the author's computer:

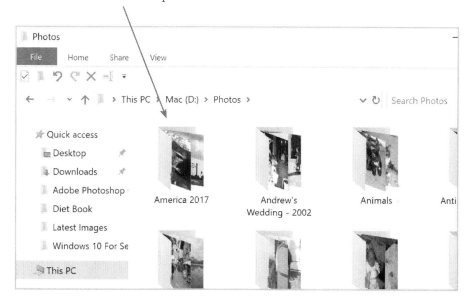

Not a single picture, i.e. file, is to be seen. They are all located in subfolders. To get to a specific file, you have to open the subfolder. You may then find that there are subfolders in the first subfolder – just keep clicking your way through them until you find the required file.

If you don't know the name of the folder that contains the wanted file then things get more difficult. You have two options here: either do a search using the search utility, or use a process of elimination to narrow it down as much as possible. Usually though, particularly if you created and saved the file yourself, you'll have a good idea of where it is.

Exploring Your Computer

An important part of exploration is keeping track of where you are, and have been – otherwise you may end up getting lost. This is no less true when exploring a computer.

To this end, File Explorer provides the Address bar. This shows the address of the currently open folder. As you move from that folder to a subfolder and then to yet another subfolder, the address of each of these folders is added to the address bar. This is demonstrated below:

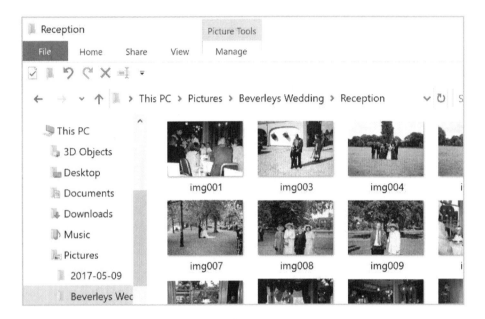

Here, we have had to open four folders to get to the required file. We opened **File Explorer, Pictures** in the default Quick Access folder, **Beverley's Wedding** in the Pictures folder and finally **Reception** in the Beverley's Wedding folder.

So you can see that the address bar shows quite clearly the route you have taken to get to your current location in Windows.

The address bar can do more though. You can use it to quickly and easily access any of the folders listed in the Address bar. You have two ways to go:

- **Retrace your steps** – clicking any folder listed in the Address bar will take you directly to that folder

- **Go anywhere** – clicking the arrow to the right of any folder in the Address bar will open a list of all the subfolders in that folder. This is demonstrated in the screenshot at the top of the next page

cont'd

Here, we have clicked the arrow to the right of Pictures – this has opened a list of all the folders in the Pictures folder. To go to any of these folders, just click on it. Other navigational aids offered by File Explorer include:

• **Back button** – at the far-left of the Address bar you will see a backward pointing arrow. Click this to go back to the most recently opened folder

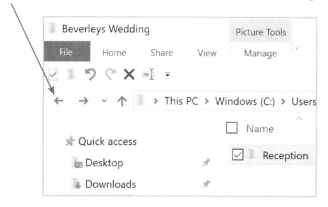

• **Forward button** – if you have already opened a subfolder, you can go back to it by clicking the forward arrow which will now be active

• **Recent locations** – next to the forward button is a down-arrow. Click this to open a list of recently opened folders

• **Up button** – next to the Recent locations button is an up-arrow. Click this to go back to the previous folder

Manage Your Files With Libraries

The Libraries feature in Windows 10 provides a central place to manage the files that are scattered throughout your computer. Instead of clicking through a bunch of directories to find the files you need, including them in a library makes for quicker access. The important thing to remember is that libraries simply gather files from different locations and display them as a single collection – they are not moved from their location. Essentially, a library is a folder full of shortcuts.

Windows starts you off with four default libraries:

- Music
- Pictures
- Videos
- Documents

As you create files of these types and click **Save As...** , on the File menu you will see the option to save the file to one of the above mentioned libraries. These will be listed on the navigation pane at the left for easy access.

You are under no obligation to use the Libraries feature but two very good reasons to do so are:

- Your documents and files will always be easy to find

- The libraries are very easy to access. Wherever you are in Windows, just click the File Explorer icon on the Taskbar and your libraries will be available on the navigation pane

Creating Libraries

There are several ways to create a new library – the one we explain here is as good as any:

1. Right-click on a folder you want to put in the library

2. Click **Include in library** and then **Create new library**

3. A new library is created and the folder is included in it. The library will be given the same name as the folder

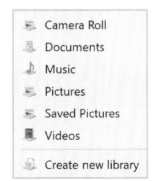

To include another folder in the library, right-click on it and click Include in library. You'll see a list of all the libraries, including any you have created yourself. Click the appropriate library and the folder will be added to it.

Find Your Data Fast With Quick Access

We've already mentioned Quick Access, which you are taken to by default when you open File Explorer. The purpose of this feature is to provide quick access to the folders you use the most. Initially, it will just show six folders: Desktop, Downloads and the four libraries. As you use the computer though, and Windows 10 learns your computing habits, it will show other folders as well. These will be the ones that you use the most.

To use the Quick Access folder:

1.   Open File Explorer

2.   In the main window, your most frequently used folders and most recently used files are displayed

If you look at the navigation pane at the left, your frequently used folders are listed there as well. These folders are all added automatically by Windows and you have no control over which are added and which aren't.

However, you can add folders to Quick Access manually. To do this, right-click the folder and click **Pin to Quick Access**.

Now open File Explorer and you will see the folder both in the navigation pane at the left and in the main folder at the right.

Open
Open folder location
Pin to Quick access
Add to VLC media player's Playlist
Browse in Adobe Bridge CS6
Play with VLC media player
Scan with Windows Defender...

Access Your Hardware With This PC

A very good way of seeing what's on your computer is to take a look at the This PC folder. To open it, click File Explorer on the Taskbar and then select **This PC** from the navigation pane. You can also just type This PC into the Taskbar search box and tap **Enter**.

At the top of the window, you'll see a ribbon toolbar (if you don't, click the down-arrow at the top-right of the window to open it). Click the **Computer** tab to reveal a number of tools and controls related to drives, networks and system management. Below, you'll see links to the default libraries and the Downloads and Desktop folders.

In the Devices and drives section, you will see all the drives connected to your computer. This is an important feature as it not only lets you access the drives, it provides an at-a-glance view of much storage space each drive has available.

The This PC folder also provides access to devices such as digital cameras, smartphones, USB flash drives, external hard drives, etc. When these are connected to the computer, an identifying icon will appear in the Devices and drives section. In the screenshot above, you can see the author's backup drive which is an external hard drive. To open these devices, just click on the relevant icon. You will then be able to access the device's storage area and transfer files to and from the computer.

Those of you who would rather File Explorer open This PC rather than Quick Access, should open File Explorer, click the **View** tab and select **Options** at the far right. On the General tab, change the value for **Open File Explorer** to **This PC** and click **OK**.

Drives and Drive Folders

Windows itself, all the files you create, and all the programs you install on the computer don't live in the ether – all this stuff is kept in a physical location known as a drive. Most drives these days are either installed inside the computer (as with a computer bought from a store) or are connected to a port on the computer's casing.

The latter are known as external drives and are used to either extend the amount of storage space available, as a backup device or as a means of transferring data between computers. As we saw on the previous page, these drives can all be accessed from the This PC folder.

When you open This PC, at the top of the list of drives (assuming there is more than one), you'll see one labeled **Windows (C:)**. This is the system drive. i.e. the one that Windows is installed on and you'll notice that it has a slightly different icon (a blue window above the drive).

Everything that happens on the computer is actually happening on this drive. It contains all your programs and files and, if it were to fail, you would be quite likely to lose it all – one very good reason to always have an up-to-date backup. Browsing a drive to see what's on it is much the same as browsing Windows itself – these devices use the same hierarchical file structure.

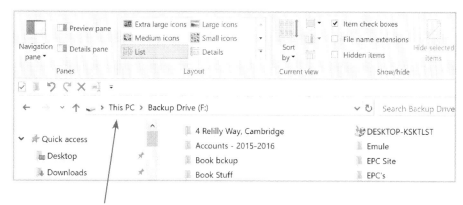

When you click a drive, it opens in the This PC view as we see here.

Configure Your System in the Control Panel

The Control Panel is a system folder which allows you to view and manipulate basic system settings and controls. For example: adding hardware, adding and removing software, controlling user accounts and changing accessibility options. Additional controls can be provided by third-party software.

To open the Control Panel, type **Control** in the Taskbar search box and tap **Enter**. It will open in the Category view. Click a category to see what tools and controls are available. Alternatively, click the **View by:** button and select **Small icons** or **Large icons** to see all the tools.

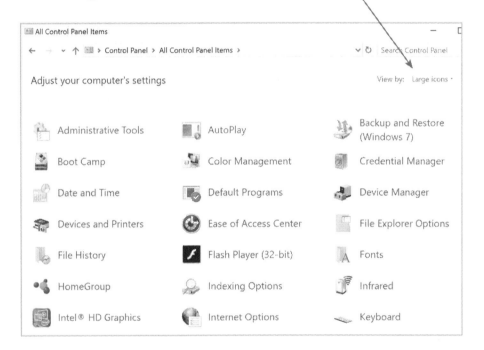

We won't go into the various options but they will enable you to configure every single part of your system. We recommend that you take a good look at what's available here and guarantee that you will discover an aspect of Windows that you never knew existed.

If you find something that you are likely to make use of, you can always create a shortcut to it by right-clicking and selecting either **Pin to Quick access** or **Pin to Start**. Note that with some, shortcuts can be placed on the Desktop only.

CHAPTER 3

Fundamentals of Windows 10

In this chapter, we take a look at the concept of windows. We explain how windows are constructed and the various elements that go to make up the typical computing window, such as menus and dialogue boxes.

We also explain the various ways in which windows can be manipulated such as moving, resizing and arranging. This is essential not only in working with them but also in terms of organisation.

How Windows are Structured

Windows are two-dimensional objects arranged on a plane called the Desktop. In a modern full-featured windowing system they can be resized, moved, hidden, restored or closed. Windows usually include other graphical objects, including a menu bar, toolbars, controls, icons and often a working area.

In the image below, which is of the Documents folder in Windows 10, we see a typical window and the elements of which it is comprised:

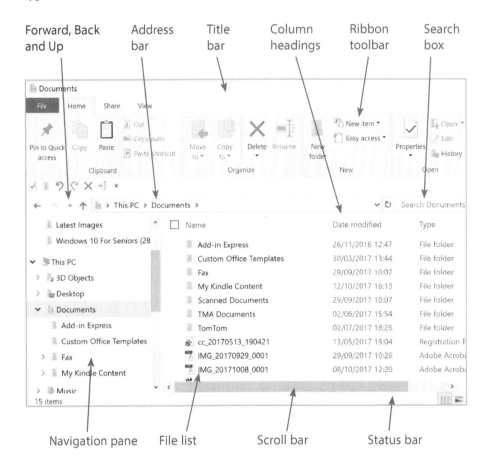

The working area of a single window usually holds only one main object. However, secondary 'child windows', such as tabs in web browsers, for example, makes it possible to have several similar documents or objects running within a single main window.

Windows can be arranged so that they do not overlap (tiled windows) or so they do overlap (overlaid windows). They can be maximised so they fill the entire screen or minimised so they don't occupy any screen space.

Types of Menu and Their Uses

A menu is a set of options presented to the user that assists in helping them find information or execute a program or function. Menus are common in graphical user interfaces (GUIs) such as Microsoft Windows and the Apple Mac operating systems. They are also employed in some speech recognition programs. Menus come in various types that include:

- **Drop-Down Menus** – in this type of menu, clicking an item causes a list of new items to appear below that item. Clicking on one of the items in the list either executes the indicated function or generates a sub-menu

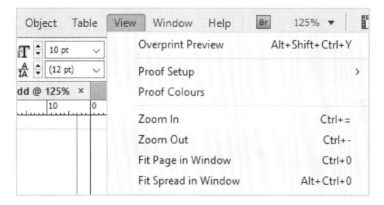

- **Fly-Out Menus** – a variant of the drop-down menus, with fly-out menus the list appears to the side of the clicked item

- **Drop-Line Menus** – with this type of menu, a bar appears below the main menu with menu options as in the example below:

- **Accordion Menus** – when you click the main menu item, the menu expands in a downwards direction. Clicking the main item again causes the menu to retract

- **Split Menus** – this is in two parts so the menu is literally 'split'. The parent items are in the main position and the child items in the sidebar.

Understanding Dialog Boxes

A dialog box is a window that allows users to perform a command, asks users a question or provides users with information or progress feedback. Typically, they are temporary and disappear once they have been acted on. A random example is shown below:

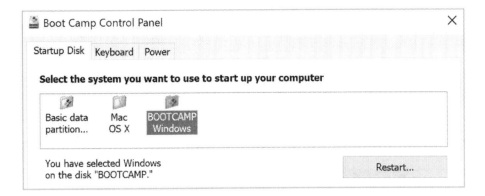

As our example shows, dialog boxes consist of a title bar at the top that specifies the command, feature or the originating program; an optional main instruction that explains the purpose of the dialog box; controls that present options and action buttons that enable the user to commit to the task.

They come in two fundamental types:

- **Modal dialog boxes** – these temporarily halt the program until the user has responded. Typical scenarios are when the program requires some additional information before it can continue, or when it wishes to confirm that the user wants to proceed with a potentially dangerous course of action

- **Modeless dialog boxes** – this type of dialog box is used when the requested information is not essential to continue, and so the window can be left open while work continues elsewhere.

On a similar vein, we have task panes. These are essentially the same as dialog boxes except that they are presented within a window instead of as a separate window. As a result, task panes have a more direct, contextual feel than dialog boxes.

Dialog boxes can have tabs and, if so, they are called tabbed dialog boxes.

Minimising and Maximising Windows

Minimising Windows

There are times when you aren't using a window but don't want to shut it down completely. The solution is to minimise the window. This removes it from the screen but doesn't close it.

To do it, just click the – button at the right of the title bar.

This will minimise the window to the Taskbar where you will see its icon is still in place as we see here:

Maximising Windows

At other times, you will want as much working area as possible. Or, you may need to enlarge a window in order to see all its contents. In both situations, you need to maximise the window.

When you do this, the window will fill the entire screen. Click this button.

Other methods of minimising, maximising and restoring are:

- **Minimise** – click the window's icon on the Taskbar

- **Maximise** – double-click the window's title bar

- **Restore** – restore a maximised window to its previous state by double-clicking its title bar. To restore a minimised window, click its icon on the Taskbar

Moving Windows

There will often be occasions when you need to move a window to a different part of the screen – usually this is when you have two or more windows open at the same time, and so need to organise your desktop.

This is the way to do it:

1. First, make sure the window is not maximised, i.e. it isn't occupying the entire screen

2. Position the mouse pointer over the window's title bar but not over the icons at the far-left and far-right of the bar

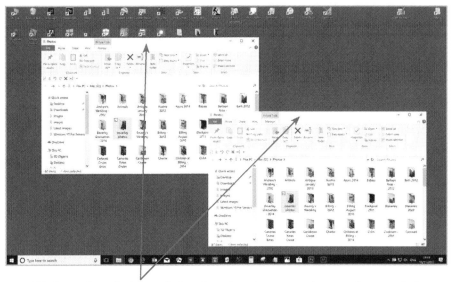

3. Click on the title bar and then keeping the mouse button depressed, drag the window to where you want it to go. You will see the window and its contents move as you drag it along

4. When the window is in the required position, release the mouse button

If you have two monitors connected to your computer thus extending your Desktop, you can drag open windows from one desktop to the other in the same way.

Resizing Windows

Sometimes you will need more precision than the Maximise and Minimise commands offer. Instead of all or nothing, you'll want something in-between, i.e. a setting of your own choice.

This can be done as follows:

1. If you want to adjust the height of the window, position the pointer on either the top or bottom edge of the window

2. If you want to adjust width of the window, position the pointer on either the left or right side of the window

3. If you want to adjust both height and width simultaneously, position the pointer in any corner of the window

Resize the width

Resize the height   Resize the width and the height

4. When the mouse pointer is correctly positioned, it turns into a two-headed arrow

5. Click the left mouse button and drag the border to resize the window as necessary

6. Release the mouse button to set the window at its new size

7. Repeat with any other borders that need to be resized

Don't forget that you can resize a window both vertically and horizontally at the same time by dragging from a corner.

Arranging Windows

Rather than resize and move your windows manually, you can take advantage of some Windows 10 tools that do the job automatically.

The procedure is:

1. Right-click on an empty area of the Taskbar to open a menu containing some useful window arrangement options

2. Select from the following three options in the menu:

- **Cascade windows** – this automatically arranges all your open windows in an overlapping arrangement that reveals the title bars of each while resizing them equally

- **Show windows stacked** – this resizes the windows equally and arranges them across the screen in rows

- **Show windows side by side** – similar to the Show windows stacked option, this arranges the windows in columns

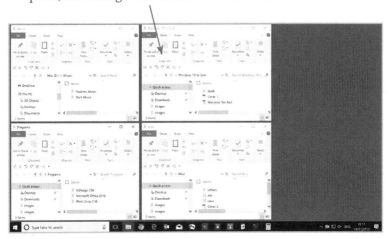

Managing Windows With Snap Assist

Snap Assist is a windows management feature that lets you arrange open windows, including maximising and resizing, simply by dragging and dropping them to different edges of the screen.

First introduced in Windows 7, the Windows 10 version also lets you snap windows to each corner of the screen. This offers more flexibility when working with multiple applications. The feature works as follows:

Snapping a Window to the Left or Right of the Screen
Position the mouse pointer on the window's title bar. Left-click and drag the window to the left or the right. When the pointer hits the screen's edge, the window snaps to it and also resizes to fill that half of the screen.

Snapping a Window Vertically
Move the mouse pointer over the window's title bar until you see it turn into a double-headed arrow. Then drag it to the top of the screen – as it hits the screen's edge, the window will maximize vertically.

Restoring a Snapped Window
If you drag a snapped window away from the edge of the screen, it will revert to its original dimensions. It won't put it back in the original position though. To do this, double-click on the window's title bar.

Snapping Multiple Windows
The Snap assist feature has another trick up it's sleeve – it lets you snap windows to each corner of the screen. This makes it possible to have the screen completely filled with four equally sized windows. Or, if you prefer, two on one half and one on the other – the permutation is up to you.

Lets say you want an arrangement similar to the one just mentioned – two windows filling the left half of the screen and another filling the right half:

1. Position the mouse pointer on the first window's title bar. Left-click and drag the window to the top-left corner of the screen

2. When you see an outline of the position the window will take appear, release the mouse button. The window will snap into position filling the top-left corner of the screen

3. Following the same procedure, drag the next window to the bottom-left corner. The window will snap into place filling the bottom-left corner

4. Drag the third window to the right edge of the screen and release it

Getting windows to snap into the corners of the screen can be a bit tricky to get the hang of initially. The secret is to do it slowly and to move the mouse pointer right into the corner.

Ways to Close Windows

Like most actions in Windows, there are a number of ways to close a window – choose the one most appropriate to the situation. If you can see the top-right corner of the window, click the X button at the far-right of the title bar.

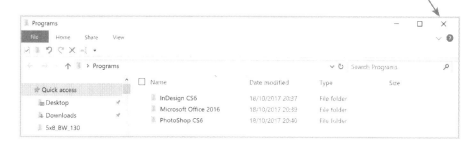

Alternatively, you can right-click on the title bar and then from the control menu, click **Close**.

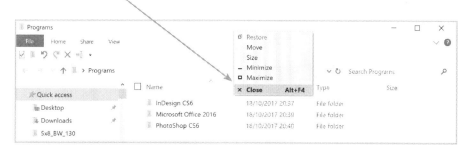

If you can't see the title bar because it is concealed or the window is minimised, hold the mouse over the window's icon on the Taskbar - you will now see a small thumbnail image of the window. Move the mouse pointer to the top of the thumbnail and click the red X button that appears.

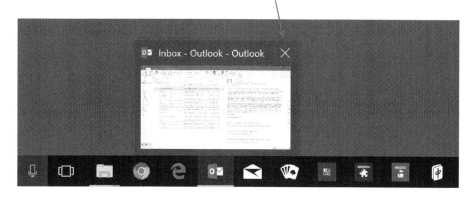

Another way to close a window from the Taskbar is to right-click the window's icon and then click **Close Window** at the bottom of the menu.

Organise Programs and Files Automatically

Every item on your computer is represented by an icon. These let you see the items, open them, close them, select them, etc, etc. The more stuff you have on your computer, the more icons there will be. Programs and files will be in two places – the Desktop and in folders. Lets see how to organise them:

The Desktop

We've already seen how desktop icons can be manually moved around the Desktop simply by dragging them to the desired position. Windows provides another, automatic, way of arranging them:

1. Right-click on an empty part of the Desktop and hold the pointer over **Sort by** to reveal a sub-menu

2. On the sub-menu, you will see options to automatically arrange the desktop icons by **Name, Size, Item type** and **Date modified**

3. Hover the mouse over **View** to see another sub-menu. This lets you set the size of the icons to **Small, Medium** or **Large**. There is also an option to **Auto arrange icons** – if you select this, any new icon created on your desktop will automatically be sorted, based on the current sorting option for desktop icons

Folders

Options for organising icons in your folders can be accessed by right-clicking in a folder. You will see the same **View** and **Sort by** menu items offering sub-menus with similar options as for the Desktop.

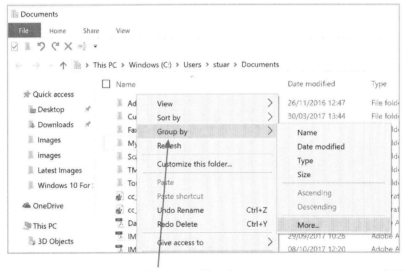

There's also an option called **Group by**. This lets you organise items in a folder by a wide range of criteria – click the **More** option to see even more options.

CHAPTER 4

Working With Files and Folders

In Chapter 4, we see how to work with files and folders. You'll learn how to create, copy, move, name and rename, delete, and search for files and folders. To do all this, Windows provides a number of tools which we will look at.

These days, computing devices are linked to the online world and a computer running Windows 10 is no different. We see how to manage your data with Microsoft's online storage facility, OneDrive.

Creating Files and Folders

Creating Files

To create a file, you first need to open the program you will use to create it. For example, if you are going to write a letter, you could use Microsoft Word.

With the program open, click **File** at the top-left of the window and select **New** – a new blank document will open.

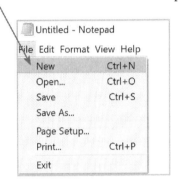 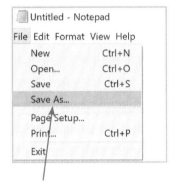

Now write your letter and, when you are finished, go back to the File menu and this time click the **Save As...** command.

It is also possible to create files with File Explorer. The procedure for this is:

1. Open the folder in which you want to create the file. A good one to use is the Documents folder provided by Windows for just this purpose (click File Explorer on the Taskbar and you will see the Documents folder in the sidebar of the File Explorer window)

2. On the ribbon toolbar at the top of the window, click **New item.** This opens a list of programs that you can use to create a file

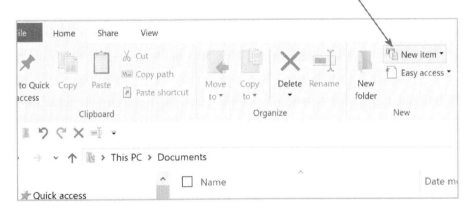

cont'd

By default, these include:

- **Shortcut** – a shortcut is basically a link, or pointer, to a program or file

- **Contact** – this creates a new contact, which is added to the People app and can be used to send email

- **Text Document** – a simple text file made using the Notepad program

Depending on what third-party applications are installed on your computer, you may also see other programs in the list.

Folders

To create a new folder, follow the same procedure as for creating a file. At Step 2, instead of clicking **New item**, click **New folder** on the toolbar.

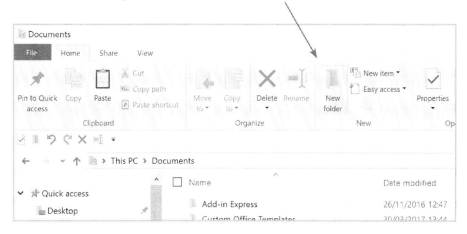

The new folder will appear at the bottom of the File Explorer window. It's name box will be open, ready for you to give it a name - see next page.

You can also create folders right on the Desktop. To do this, just right-click on an empty part of the Desktop and, from the menu that opens, select **New**. You will now see the same list of programs as at Step 2. Right at the top is an option for creating a folder.

Naming Files and Folders

Naming a File or Folder

Having created a file or folder as described on the previous page, you will now want to give it an identifying name. This is very easy to do. For example, when you click **New** > **Folder** to create a folder, you will see the following:

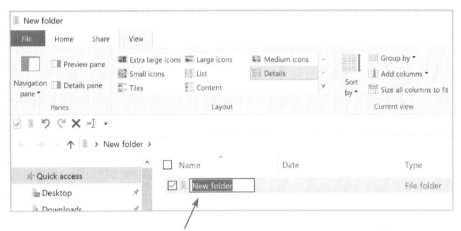

Click in the box, delete **New folder** and type in the desired name. Windows supports file names up to 255 characters so you can give it an interesting name if you want to.

All files created with a program have to be given a name. When you click the **Save as...** command to save a file, this is the point at which you will be prompted to name it.

Renaming a File or Folder

If you don't like the name of a file or folder for some reason, there are several ways to change it to something more to your liking:

- Right-click on the file or folder and click **Rename**. Then enter the new name in the box

- Select the file or folder (see the next page) in File Explorer and then click **Rename** on the ribbon toolbar at the top of the window

- Select the file or folder and then press the **F2** key. The Rename box will appear – delete the old name and enter the new one

Windows will accept most keyboard characters, spaces included. However, it will not accept any names that include * | \ : < > ? /.

Selecting Files and Folders

To be able to work with files and folders, i.e. move them around and all the other things that are possible, you need to be able to select them. This can be done as follows:

1. Open the folder that contains the required file or folder

2. Hold the mouse pointer over the item's icon – the line it is on will be highlighted in blue indicating it has been selected

You can then carry out whatever action you want with the file or folder. However, while this will be OK for dealing with a single file or folder, it won't be so clever when you have a whole bunch of them to handle.

A typical example is when you have a number of pictures that you want to download from your digital camera to the computer – moving these one by one will be a slow and tedious procedure. A much better way is to move them all at the same time.

To do this, you need to select all the files as a group. Having done so, you can download them with one command. There are actually several ways to select items as a group. These include:

*   **Selecting consecutive items** – in a folder where all the files are listed consecutively, select the first one by hovering on it, then press the **Shift** key and, with it held down, go to the last file in the folder and click it. Now release the **Shift** key. All the files in between the first and last will now be selected

*   **Selecting nonconsecutive items** – in the opposite scenario where the files are not listed in any sort of order you need to do it a different way. Select the first file, press and hold the **Ctrl** key, and then click the required files. Finally, release the **Ctrl** key – all the files will be selected

*   **Select all command** – make sure the ribbon toolbar at the top of the folder is open and then click **Select all** at the right of the toolbar

*   **Box them in** – with the left mouse button depressed, drag a rectangle around the files you want to select

Having selected some files, you can deselect them if necessary by simply clicking in an empty part of the folder.

Copying/Moving Files and Folders

There are many reasons why you may want to copy or move a file or folder to a different location. With regard to copying, one obvious example is to create a backup copy of an important file. As with so many Windows actions, there are a number of ways to do this. One method is to open the folder containing the file to be moved and position it next to the folder the file is to be moved to:

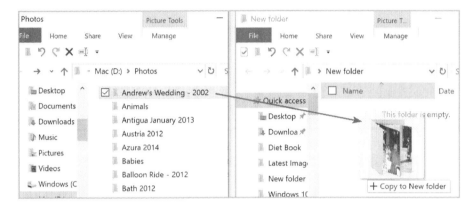

With both folders open, left-click on the file and simply drag it across to the destination folder. When you see **Copy to xxx folder** appear below the file, release it – it will now be copied to the destination folder.

The same method can be used to move a file as well. In this case, you need to right-click on the file and drag it across. When you release it, a menu will appear offering **Move here, Copy here** and **Create shortcuts here** options. Click the **Move here** option to move the file across.

When it is not convenient to have the folders arranged alongside each other, you can use the ribbon toolbar. Open the folder containing the file to be moved and select it. On the toolbar, select the **Home** tab and then click either the **Move to** or **Copy to** button. A menu of commonly used folders, such as the Desktop, Music and Pictures will open.

Alternatively, you can click **Choose location** at the bottom and browse to the destination folder. Click it and the file will be copied/moved to it.

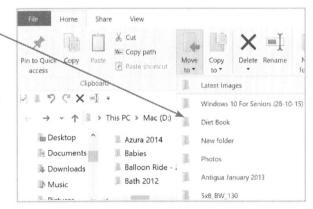

Quickly View a File With File Preview

The procedure for seeing what's in a file is to double-click on the file's icon, which opens it in the program that was used to create it. If you don't want the bother of doing this though and just need a quick glance at the file, Windows provides the answer in the form of it's File preview feature.

Preview a file as follows:

1. Open File Explorer

2. Click the **View** tab

3. Click **Preview pane**

4. Browse to the file you want to preview and select it

5. A preview of the file appears in the Preview pane at the right side of the window

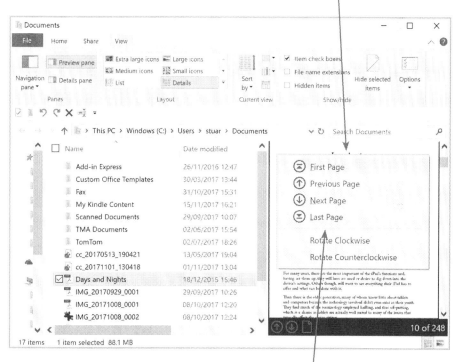

6. Right-clicking on the preview may reveal some options depending on the type of the file. In the example above, we see a PDF file that has several pages, so the right-click menu offers First, Previous, Next and Last page options

Note that not all types of file are supported by the Preview feature. In this case, you will see a message saying 'No preview available'.

How to Delete Stuff You No Longer Need

Given the enormous capacities of current drives, lack of storage space is much less of an issue than it used to be. That said, you can still find yourself running out of space, particularly if you keep a lot of image and video files on the computer. Another issue that can result from too much clutter is that of the computer's performance – it can be adversely effected. You may also get spurious errors, reboots and other problems.

So while you may have plenty of space on your drive, it is still a good idea to get rid of stuff you don't need. Deleting files is easy enough to do – just right-click on the file and click **Delete**. If you have a bunch of files that need showing the door, select them as a group as we described on page 55 before clicking **Delete**.

However, you should know that files deleted in this way are not actually deleted – they are placed in a system folder called the Recycle Bin. You'll find this folder on the Desktop at the top-left. The purpose of the Recycle Bin is to give you a chance to get a file back if you change your mind or if you deleted it accidentally.

Should you wish to recover a file, open the Recycle Bin, right-click on the file and click **Restore** – it will be moved back to its original location. Another way, assuming it has just been deleted, is to press **Ctrl + Z**. You will also see options on the ribbon toolbar that let you restore files.

When you are sure that a particular file, or bunch of files, really has to go, the following actions will remove it from the computer completely.

- Open the Recycle Bin, right-click on the file and select **Delete**

- To delete all the files in the Recycle Bin in one go, right-click on the Recycle Bin icon and click **Empty Recycle Bin** – everything will go

- On the ribbon toolbar, click **Empty Recycle Bin**

A more drastic method of file deletion involves a procedure known as 'formatting'. This is carried out on a drive and it basically deletes the existing file system on the drive and replaces it with a new one. The process also wipes the drive clean of all data.

To do it, open the **This PC** folder and right-click on the drive. From the menu that appears, click **Format...** After a moment a window will appear offering various formatting options. Click the **Start** button at the bottom.

Note that the C: drive on which Windows is installed cannot be formatted for obvious reasons. All other drives can be though.

Reduce File Size With Compression

File compression is a process of 'packaging' a file (or files) to reduce its size. It works by minimising redundancy in the file's code. Compression software makes it possible to take many files and compress them into a single file, which is smaller than the combined size of the originals.

Most of the files you download from the Internet, such as apps and email attachments, arrive on your computer in a compressed state. Windows PCs have a built-in file compression system that compresses and decompresses these files automatically without the user ever knowing about it.

However, file compression is also available for the user. For example, you may want to reduce the size of a folder containing pictures. Or, you can compress the contents of an entire drive in order to reclaim some storage space. There are two ways to do it:

1.   Right-click on the folder or drive that you want to compress

2.   At the bottom of the menu, click **Properties**

3.   On the General tab, click the **Advanced** button

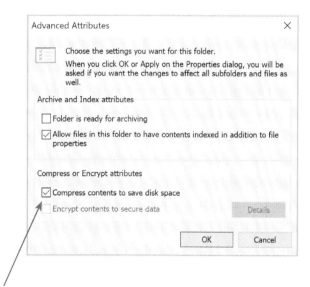

4.   Check the **Compress contents to save disk space** box

If you decide to compress a drive, be aware that depending on the size of the drive, the procedure can take hours. Also, if any files or programs on the drive are open, they will bring the compression procedure to a halt.

Using Windows 10's Search Facilities

The typical computer is literally stuffed to the gills with thousands upon thousands of files. Finding something specific would be a very difficult, if not impossible, task were it not for the search facilities built in to Windows.

When doing a search, you basically have two ways to go:

Computer-wide Searches

If you have no idea of where a particular file, application or setting is located, then you need to use the search box on the Taskbar. Click in the box and just type your query – as you type, results will appear above.

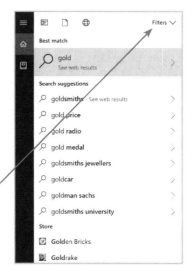

When you look at them, you'll see that they are not taken just from the computer – the feature searches the Windows Store and the Internet as well.

So you will probably need to click the Filters button at the top-right. This enables you to streamline your search and will almost always result in a more manageable and relevant list of results.

Folder Searches

If you know a file is in a particular folder but can't be bothered to search through it, just type your search term in the search box that is at the top-right of every File Explorer window:

The results appear in the main body of the window – just click one to open it.

Ways to Print a File

Printing a document or picture is very easy to do and can be done in two ways – with the program used to create the file or with File Explorer.

With the Program

Open the document or picture to be printed and then click **File** (at the top-left of the window in most programs). On the File menu, select the **Print** option – you will then see the Print dialogue box as shown below:

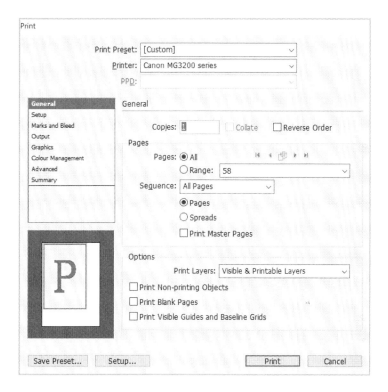

The print options offered vary depending on the type of document but will always include a list of available printers, a text box to specify the number of copies required and a page range control that lest you specify which parts of the document are to be printed.

File Explorer

Printing a file with File Explorer is even easier. All you have to do is right-click on the file regardless of where it is and, from the menu, select the Print option. The Print dialogue box will open as above – specify your print requirements and then click **OK** to print the file.

When printing images, you will see a different range of options than with text documents. These will include paper size, print quality, paper type, number of copies, etc.

Writing Files to a CD or DVD Disc

Writing (burning) files to a disc used to be a somewhat complicated procedure thanks to the proliferation of disc types, i.e. CD, CD-R, CD-RW and DVD.

Windows 8 however, and now Windows 10, has made the process much simpler. In fact, it is no different now than saving a file on any other type of file-storage medium, such as a hard drive or flash drive.

This is assuming of course, that you are still using this somewhat outmoded type of data storage/transfer. If, for whatever reason, you are:

1. Place the disc into the disc drive

2. Windows will take a few moments to examine it

3. Open This PC and look for the drive's icon – it will be showing the type of disc, its capacity and the amount of free space on the disc

4. Click the drive's icon to open the **Burn a Disc** screen

5. We suggest you select the first option **Like a USB flash drive**. This will let you use the disc in exactly the same way as you would a hard drive – saving, deleting, editing, etc

6. Windows will now format the disc to create a file system on it

When the format procedure is done, you can then use the disc. Files can be added to it in two ways:

1. Click the drive's icon in This PC to open the disc. Now just drag the files you want to burn on to the window and release them

2. Open File Explorer and browse to the required file. Click the **Share** tab and then click **Burn to disc**

3. A window will open showing the progress of the file transfer. When completed, click the drive to open the disc and see the files on it

Configure How Folders Look and Function

By default, folders are presented in a certain way when opened. For example, the ribbon toolbar is minimised. However, you have quite a few options with regard to changing how your folders look and operate.

1. Your first move is to maximise the ribbon toolbar by clicking the little down-arrow at the top-right corner of any folder below the X button

2. Next, click the **View** tab to reveal the available options

We won't go into all the ribbon toolbar settings but they make it possible to customise your folders in numerous ways. You can close the navigation pane, activate preview and details panes, alter the size of item icons and sort your files in a number of ways. You can also add columns that provide more information with regard to the files, activate check boxes that make it easier to select files, and configure items to show their file type next to their name.

Click the **Options** button at the far-right and a Folder Options window will open as we see here.

This offers even more configuration options. For example, you can set File Explorer to open at This PC rather than Quick Access.

It is also possible to set folders to open in their own window.

You can set the mouse to open items with a single click rather than a double click.

At the bottom are various Privacy options that will be useful for some people.

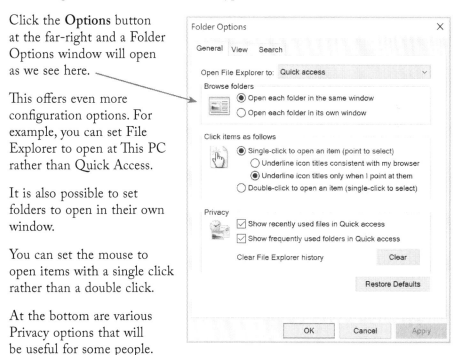

For example, clearing File Explorer's history so another user won't be able to see what files and folders they've been accessing.

Save Data Online With OneDrive

The Internet is now ubiquitous in most people's lives so it's no surprise to find that Windows 10 is in on the act as well. It is actually, to a large degree, built around the online world. This is the reason you are urged at almost every turn while using Windows 10 to sign up for a Microsoft account if you haven't already got one.

Having a Microsoft account allows you and Windows 10 to use various online services; one of which is the ability to synchronise your computer's settings with other devices that are linked to that account.

Another benefit is that you can make use of Microsoft's online file storage facility, OneDrive. This is basically a free online drive on which you can store whatever type of files and data you wish. You are given 5GB of space, which is an ample amount in which to store important documents.

Setting Up OneDrive
On the Start Menu, scroll down to **OneDrive** under the letter O and click to open it..

1. The **Welcome to OneDrive** screen will open. Click the **Get started** button

2. The next window asks you to sign in to your Microsoft account

3. You are introduced to your OneDrive folder. At the bottom of the screen, you will see the folder's location on the computer. If you want to use a different folder, click the **Change** button and browse to and select the required folder

cont'd

4. The next window shows you a list of system folders whose contents will be synced to OneDrive. Next to each is a checkbox that lets you deselect the folder if you don't wish it's contents to be synced. When you are happy, click **Next**. OneDrive is now set up on your computer.

Using OneDrive

The OneDrive feature keeps all its data in one folder called, not surprisingly, OneDrive. Access it as follows:

1. Click the **Start menu** button and scroll down to, and click, **OneDrive**

2. Another way is to open File Explorer and look at the navigation pane. Below Quick Access, you'll see OneDrive – click to open it. Its contents, which initially will be just be the default system folders, will be displayed in the main window on the right. Should you wish to do so, you can add more folders – you aren't restricted to the default ones

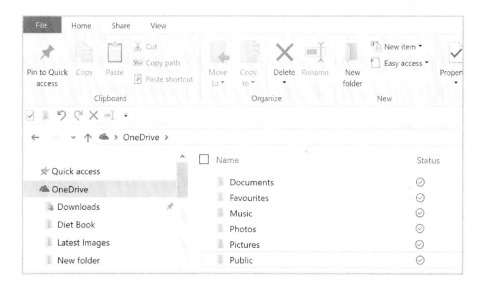

You are now ready to start using OneDrive by adding files to be stored and synchronised online. Proceed as follows:

1. With the OneDrive folder open as above, drag your files from their current folder and drop them in either the OneDrive folder itself or one of the subfolders

2. Alternatively, having created the file, go to **Save as...** on the menu, browse to the OneDrive folder and save it there

Using OneDrive Online

As OneDrive is an online service, it can be accessed via your web browser as well as your computer. To do this:

1. Go to **www.onedrive.live.com** and sign in to your Microsoft account. You will then be able to access OneDrive

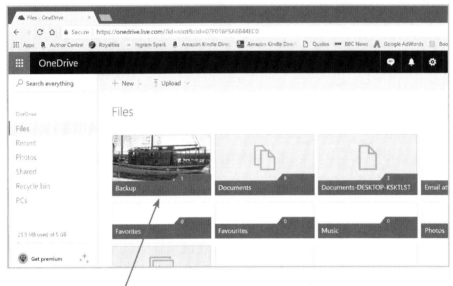

2. The online version can be used in much the same way as on your computer – creating new files and folders, moving, copying, deleting and more. All changes you make will be replicated on your computer

OneDrive Settings

OneDrive's settings are tucked away in Windows. To access them, click **Settings** on the Start menu and then **System.**

Click **Notifications & actions** and then scroll down to **Get notifications from these senders.** Next to **OneDrive,** click the switch to **On.**

Now look in the Taskbar's Notification area for the OneDrive icon. If you don't see it, click the up-arrow at the left to show hidden icons. Right-click on the OneDrive icon and select **Settings**.

CHAPTER 5

Applications That Come With Windows

The term 'App' is short for application and is rapidly replacing the more traditional 'computer program'.

Windows 10 comes with a number of pre-installed apps which cover the main functions computers are used for. You will, however, almost certainly want to install your own apps at some point. These can be downloaded from the Windows Store and other sources as we'll see.

In this chapter, we show you how to find, download and install apps from the Store, and how to manage and organise them.

Apps and Programs Explained

As we mentioned in the introduction to this chapter, the term 'App' is a relatively new one and has largely, but not completely, replaced 'program'. Its origins are in the world of smartphones and tablet computers, and it refers to the small and basic applications that are used on these devices.

However, Microsoft has seen fit to now label all the programs it supplies with Windows as apps, so apps they will be! They offer a lot more apps in the Windows Store should the default ones not be sufficient for your needs.

There are also literally thousands of traditional programs out there. Just so there's no confusion, we'll explain the differences between Windows apps and the older type of program:

Windows Apps
Windows 10, and its predecessor Windows 8, come with a number of built-in apps that cover the main functions of computers. To see a complete list of these apps in Windows 10, open the Start menu and scroll down. You will also see some of them on the right-hand side of the Start menu.

When you click them, they open in a minimalist window that is totally unlike that of traditional computer programs. The apps are easily recognizable by their brightly coloured tile-like appearance.

Programs
Traditional computer programs (the Adobe InDesign program used to write this book in the example below), are identifiable by their icons, rather than a coloured tile as with apps. Also, when you open them, the window they run in will be much more involved and busy in terms of menus, toolbars and graphics.

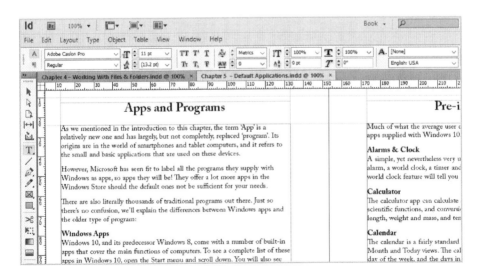

Apps Pre-installed in Windows 10

Much of what the average user does on his/her computer will be covered by the apps supplied with Windows 10. They include:

Alarms & Clock
A simple, yet nevertheless very useful, app that provides four functions: an alarm, a world clock, a timer and a stopwatch. Just type in a location and the world clock feature will tell you the local time.

Calculator
The calculator app can calculate a wide range of data. It offers standard and scientific functions, and conversions that include energy, programming, volume, length, weight and mass and temperature.

Calendar
The calendar is a fairly standard affair that offers Day, Work week, Week, Month and Today views. The calendar's settings let you change the colours, first day of the week and the days in the work week.

Camera
Intended for people with a Windows 10 smartphone or tablet, the Camera app has a number of useful features, including 4K video recording, auto-HDR, Rich Capture and a Dynamic Flash mode.

Cortana
Cortana is Windows 10's personal assistant. It will find things on your PC, manage your calendar, find files and more. The more you use Cortana, the more personalised your experience with it will be.

Groove Music
For music aficionados, the Groove Music app lets you organise your music collection by album, artist and song. You can create playlists, buy music and add your music to OneDrive to play anywhere.

Maps
This useful app opens showing your current location. With it, you can view maps from literally every part of the globe. You can get directions, 3D views of famous cities and find hotels.

Microsoft Edge
The default Internet browser in Windows 10, Edge replaces the now defunct Windows Explorer. Slick and fast, this new browser does everything that Windows Explorer did and more.

Money

Location-based, the Money app provides real-time information that lets you keep on top of your financial affairs. Keep an eye on global stock markets, create watchlists, convert currencies and much more.

Films & TV

A simple app that lets you manage all the video content on your computer. This includes home videos, TV shows and movies downloaded from the Windows Store. You can also buy from here.

News

Another real-time app, the News app keeps you abreast of what's going on, not just in your part of the world, but globally. Topics covered include sport, trending, entertainment, money and fitness.

OneDrive

The OneDrive app opens your free online storage. With it you can store, sync and share data with other people. Files on OneDrive can be accessed directly from a web browser or from your computer.

OneNote

This is a note taking application and is part of the Microsoft Office Suite. With it, you can create notebooks, insert pictures, tables and draw. Your notes can also be saved on OneDrive.

People

A very straightforward app, People is your personal address book. In it, you can keep the contact details, including addresses, phone numbers and email addresses of the people in your life.

Photos

Also simple and straightforward, the Photos app is for viewing your pictures. You can use it to organise them in collections and albums, view in a slideshow, enhance, edit and print.

Settings

If you need to change any of your computer's default settings, the Settings app is the place to go. With it, you can configure a range of settings including System, Devices, Network and Security.

Store

Store takes you to Microsoft's Windows Store. Here, you will be able to browse through literally thousands of apps across all genres and buy any that will be useful. Some apps can be downloaded for free.

Voice Recorder
The Voice Recorder is an app you can use to record audio. You can use it alongside other apps, which allows you to record sound while you continue working on your computer.

Weather
This provides up-to-date weather forecasts for literally anywhere in the world. It also provides historical weather, shows weather patterns and trends, and the latest weather news from around the world.

Xbox
Xbox connects you to the world of online gaming. Stream your Xbox games to any Windows 10 computer and play new games optimised specifically for Windows 10.

Working With Windows 10 Apps

In Window 8, there was a lot of controversy over the way the default apps looked and operated. When you opened one, you were immediately switched to the Start screen – this made it difficult to use them alongside traditional desktop programs. Not only that, they insisted on taking up the entire screen.

For these reasons, and others, Windows 8 and 8.1 were not popular. With Windows 10, it seems that Microsoft has taken heed of the criticisms (or declining sales!) and come up with a more sensible approach.

For starters, Windows 10 apps now open directly on the Desktop. Furthermore, they open in a traditional style window that can be moved and resized.

To move a Windows 10 app around the screen, click on the title bar and then drag it to the new location

The apps's window can be extended in any direction by dragging the appropriate border. You can resize it vertically and horizontally at the same time by dragging the corners

Toolbars and Menus

Just as with a traditional program, right-clicking on the title bar opens a menu offering Restore, Move, Size, Minimise, Maximise and Close options. These provide another way of manipulating your apps.

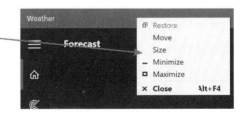

cont'd

Unlike traditional programs that always almost have a visible toolbar at the top from where all the program's options and features can be accessed, Windows 10 apps are more discreet. The Groove Music app is a typical example:

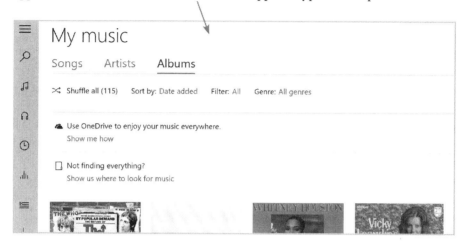

As with many of the apps, when opened, Groove Music presents a narrow toolbar down the left-hand side. If you click the icon at the top-left, the toolbar expands to show the text labels for the various buttons.

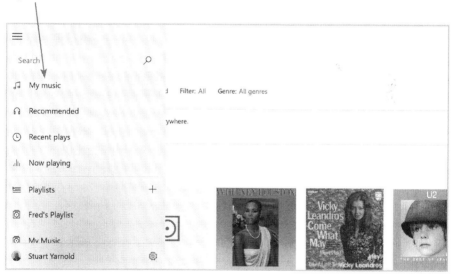

As you move about in apps, you will notice an arrow button appear at the top-left corner – click it to go back to the previous page. Also on the toolbar will be a Settings button; click it to access the app's settings screen.

With other apps, right-clicking on the window will open a menu of options.

Where to Find Your Apps

In Windows 10, all apps installed on the computer can be accessed by clicking the **Start menu** button at the left of the Taskbar. When the Start menu opens, on the left, you will see an alphabetical list of the apps installed on the computer as we see below:

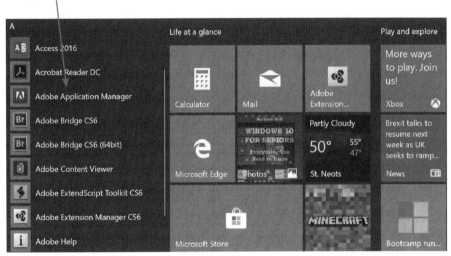

The list also includes any traditional programs that you may have installed yourself.

To open one, just double-click on its icon – its window will open on the Desktop, as with the Wordpad program shown below:

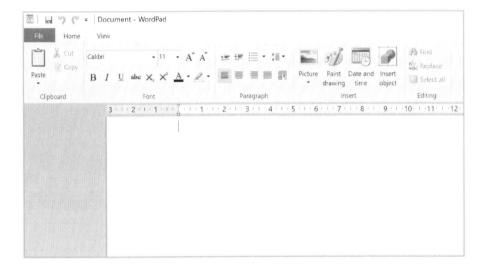

Viewing All Your Apps and Programs

As explained on the previous page, the Start menu lists all the applications installed on your computer. On the left you see the entire list while the tiles on the right show the ones you use the most, or have pinned there yourself (see page 77 for how to pin apps). You will notice that traditional computer programs may just show a folder rather than a program icon as with apps. In this case, you will see a down-arrow to the right of the folder as we see here.

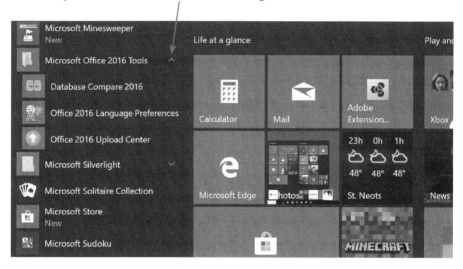

Click the arrow and you will then see the program's launching icon. Often, you will see other programs associated with the main program as well, as we see in the screenshot above where the Microsoft Office 2016 folder has been clicked.

Another way to view apps in the Start menu is to click on a letter heading. This opens an alphabetical grid – click on a letter to go to the apps listed under it.

Click the **clock** icon at the front of the grid to revert to the beginning of the list and the **globe** icon at the end to go to the end of the list.

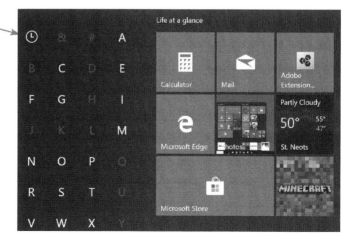

75

cont'd

You can also view all your apps and programs in the Control Panel. Type **Control Panel** in the Taskbar search box and tap **Enter**. The Control Panel will open in the Category view.

Click on **Category** at the top-right of the window and select **Small icons** from the menu that opens. Now click **Programs and features** to open the window shown below:

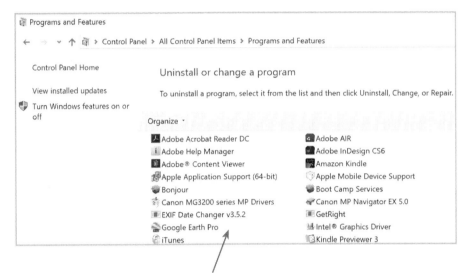

This shows you an alphabetical list of all the apps, programs and drivers installed on the computer. By clicking **Change your view** at the top-right of the window and then clicking **Details**, you will also be able to see when your apps and programs were installed, their size and version number.

Just one example of when this information can be very useful is when you are thinking about upgrading a program.

Pinning Apps For Quick Access

Windows 10 starts you off with some default apps placed at the right of the Start menu where they can be quickly and easily accessed. You will also see three apps on the Taskbar at the immediate right of the search box.

Should you want to do so, you can add your own apps, or replace the default ones, in both locations. The procedure is known as Pinning. The apps you pin to the Start menu should be ones you use frequently.

Do it as described below:

1. Click the **Start** button to open the Start menu

2. Right-click on the app to be pinned

3. To pin the app to the Start menu, click **Pin to Start**

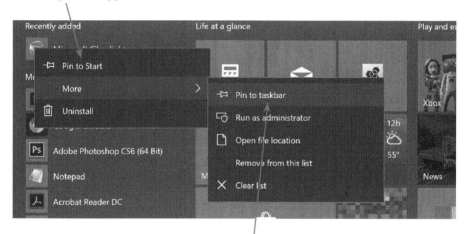

4. To pin the app to the Taskbar, click **Pin to taskbar**

Apps that are open and thus on the Taskbar can also be pinned there. The method for doing this is to right-click on the app's taskbar icon and then click **Pin to taskbar**.

Should you decide to unpin an app from either the Start menu or Taskbar, right-click on it and then click **Unpin from Start** or **Unpin from taskbar** respectively.

The Windows Store

When you want to add more functionality to your computer, the Windows Store is one place to go. Here, you will find not just apps but also games, films, TV shows and music. We'll concentrate on the apps for now.

To open the Store, click the **Store** icon on the Taskbar. On the opening screen, click **Apps** on the menu bar at the top of the window:

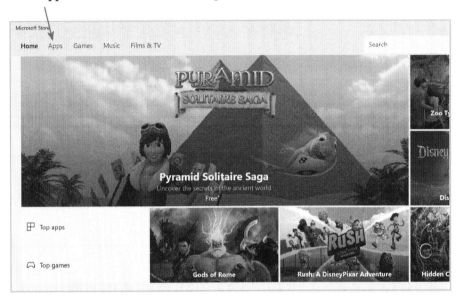

Scrolling down the Apps page, you'll see several sections that include: Apps that we've picked for you, Top free apps, Top paid apps, Best-rated apps, Trending apps, Collections and Categories. If any of these are of interest, click the **Show all** link at the right of the section to see more. If you have an idea of what you are looking for, click Categories at the bottom.

Categories		
Books & reference	Business	Developer tools
Entertainment	Food & dining	Government & politics
Kids & family	Lifestyle	Medical
Music	Navigation & maps	News & weather

Click the category you are interested in. A list of related apps will open in a new window.

cont'd

Click on one to see what it's about.

At the top, you'll see a brief description of what the apps does – click the **More** button for more details. Below that is the price of the app, followed by some screenshots of the app in action, it's system requirements, additional information, age rating, and ratings and reviews.

If you click on the screenshots, they'll open full-screen giving you a better view. Reading the ratings and reviews will give you a good idea of whether or not the app is good for its stated purpose.

Buying and Installing Apps

If you decide you want a particular app, proceed as follows:

1. Open the app's details screen and click the **Buy** button

2. A window will open asking you to sign in by entering your Microsoft account password

3. A **Buy app** window will now open. Enter the requested details and then click the **Buy** button. The fee will be deducted from the credit card registered to your account. Some apps, of course, are free, in which case you won't have to go through the payment process

4. The app is now downloaded to your computer – you will see a progress bar on the screen. When the download is complete, it will be installed automatically – you don't have to do a thing

5. Still on the app's details screen, you will now see an **Open** button. Click it to open the app

6. Alternatively, open the Start menu. At the top, above the **Most used** section, you will now see a **Recently added** section. Your new app will be listed here – click to open it

After a while, the app will disappear from the Recently added section. From that point, you will have to access it by scrolling down to where it is listed under the appropriate letter in the Start menu. Initially, it will have a **New** tag appended to it.

A large proportion of software these days is downloaded from the Internet. However, should you have a program supplied on a CD or DVD disc, the installation procedure will be:

1. Place the disc in your computer's CD/DVD drive

2. Windows 10 will automatically look for an installation program on the disc. If it finds one, a pop-up window should open asking you to **Click to choose what happens with this disc**. If it does, click the window

3. If you don't see the pop-up window, open the This PC folder and click on the **CD/DVD drive** to access the disc

4. The installation program should now open. If it doesn't, look for it on the disc – it will be labeled **Setup** or **Install** – click it

5. Follow the prompts to install the program – the procedure may vary slightly from program to program

In the case of a program downloaded from the Internet, do the following:

1. When you click the Download button, you will see the following dialogue box at the bottom of the browser (assuming you are using Edge)

2. Click Run. This initiates a security scan after which you will see a message asking **Do you want this app to make changes to your device?** Click **Yes**. You will now see the program's installation screen open - just follow the prompts to install it

Keeping Track of Your App Purchases

Buying apps can become an addictive pastime and you may at some point wish to review what you have already bought. Trying to do it from the Start menu will be tedious and time-consuming, so you will be pleased to know there is a better way.

1. Open the Windows Store and click the button at the far top-right of the browser window

2. In the menu that opens, click **Purchased**

3. You will now be asked to sign in to your Microsoft account

4. Thet account will open in a browser window at the **Order history** page where you can see exactly what you have bought and when

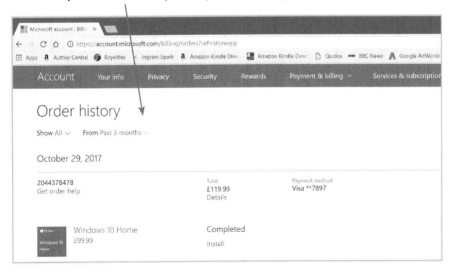

Uninstalling Apps From Your System

The default apps supplied with Windows - Photos, Calculator, Calendar, etc, cannot be uninstalled. The only thing you can do with these is to remove them from the Start menu as we describe on page 77. However, you can uninstall apps you have installed yourself. The procedure is:

1. Open the Start menu and right-click on the app to be uninstalled

2. The right-click menu will show an **Uninstall** option – click it

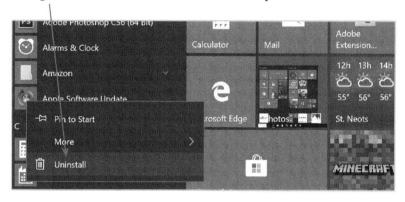

3. You'll now see a warning message stating **This app and its related info will be uninstalled** – click the **Uninstall** button to remove the app from the computer

However, if you are uninstalling a program, such as Microsoft Word, the procedure will be slightly different. At Step 2, clicking the **Uninstall** button will open the Programs and Features utility in the Control Panel, as shown below:

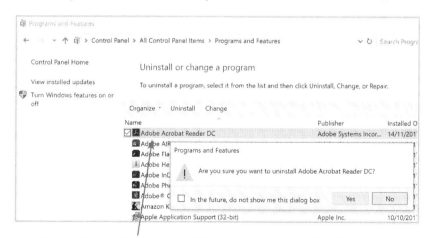

Locate the app in the Programs and Features window, right-click on it and click the **Uninstall** button. You will see a warning message asking if you are sure you want to uninstall it – click **Yes** and the program will be uninstalled.

Live Tiles and How to Use Them

As already mentioned, the default apps supplied with Windows 10 look somewhat different to the traditional Windows programs. Instead of each having a unique icon, they are all represented by a coloured tile.

Some of these tiles are 'live' meaning that instead of just showing an unchanging colour, they display real-time information. A typical example is the News app as we see here:

By default, if an app tile has live functionality, it is activated. Should you not want this, you can turn it off by right-clicking on the tile and clicking **More > Turn live tile off.**

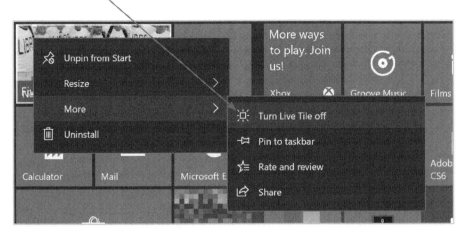

Apps that have live functionality are: Mail, People, Calendar, Photos, Groove Music, News, Sport and Money.

Note that with some of these apps, it will be necessary to set up a Microsoft account before the live functionality is available.

CHAPTER 6

Customise the Way Windows Looks and Acts

In Chapter 6, we see how to customise your computing environment to reflect your personality, mode of working and preferences.

You will learn how to alter the visual look of Windows by changing the Desktop and Lock Screen backgrounds, the size of screen elements, the sounds it emits, accessibility options and much more.

Wallpaper the Desktop and Lock Screen

One of the first things that most people do when using a new operating system is to change the Desktop's background, or wallpaper as it is more commonly known. It is also possible to change the Lock screen's background as well.

Desktop Background
To change the Desktop background, do the following:

1. Right-click on an empty part of the Desktop and click **Personalize**

2. The Personalization window opens – click **Background** on the left

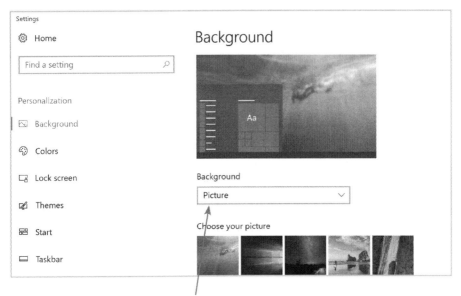

In the drop-down box under Background, you'll see three options: Picture, Solid colour and Slideshow. Select the former and you'll be offered a choice of five default pictures. Below, you'll see a **Browse** button. Clicking this will open the Pictures folder in File Explorer. You can either select one from here or browse to another location and select one from there.

Select the Solid colour option to open a list of 24 colours. Just click one to set it as the Desktop colour. Click Custom colour to mix your own colour.

The Slideshow option lets you play a slideshow on the Desktop. Click the **Browse** button to select albums from which the pictures for the slideshow will be taken. You can choose different time periods for the pictures to change.

At the bottom of the window, you can choose a fit if you have selected a picture as the background. Options include Fill, Fit, Stretch, Tile, Center and Span.

Lock Screen Background

To change how the Lock screen looks:

1. In the Personalization window, click **Lock screen** at the left

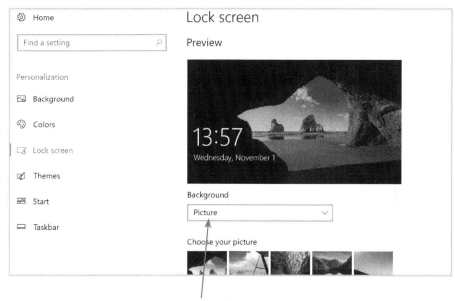

2. Click in the box under Background and you will see three options: Windows spotlight (this is the default Lock screen background), Picture and Slideshow. Click the **Browse** button or the **Add a folder** button to select the required picture, or pictures, for the latter two options

Something that is available for the Lock screen but not for the Desktop is notifications – these provide real-time updates on various events. The Lock screen Personalization window lets you specify which apps you want to show these notifications.

You will be able to choose one app to show detailed information, and up to seven to show basic information. Just click in the + boxes to open the list of apps on your computer.

Right at the bottom of the window, you'll see a **Screen timeout settings** link. This lets you specify the time after which the PC's screen is turned off, and after which it is put to sleep.

Set Up a Screensaver

A screensaver is a simple program that fills the screen with moving images or patterns when the computer is not in use. Originally designed to prevent phosphor burn-in on CRT and plasma monitors, screensavers are now used primarily for entertainment, security or to display system status information.

To set up a screensaver on your Windows 10 computer:

1. Click the **Start** button and then **Settings** on the Start menu. The Settings app opens - click **Personalization** and then **Lock screen**

2. At the bottom of the Lock screen page, click **Screen saver settings** to open the window shown below:

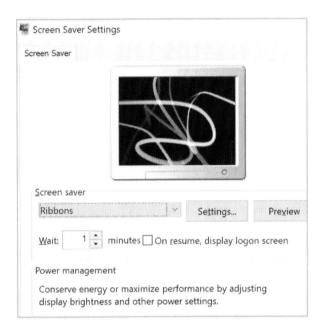

3. Click the drop-down box to select the required screensaver. As you do, you will see a mini-preview in the small screen. To see a full-screen preview, click the **Preview** button. Move the mouse to end the preview

4. Some of the screensavers have settings that can be adjusted. To see what these are, select the screensaver and then click the **Settings** button

5. Below the drop-down box, you'll see a **Wait:** box. If you want to specify a time before the screensaver activates, enter it here. You can either type in the required time or set it with the up/down arrows.

Windows 10 does not supply many screensavers. However, you can download many more from the Internet. Most are far more complex and useful as well.

Quick Customisation With Themes

On a related note, we have Themes. A theme is a combination of pictures, colours and sounds. It includes a Desktop background, a screensaver, a window border colour and a sound scheme. Some themes also include desktop icons and mouse pointers.

Themes provide a quick way of customising the look and sound of your computer. Several themes are provided with Windows 10 but if you don't like any of these, you can find literally hundreds online.

To see what Windows 10 has to offer:

1. Right-click on an empty part of the Desktop and click **Personalize**

2. The Personalisation window opens – click **Themes** at the left of the screen

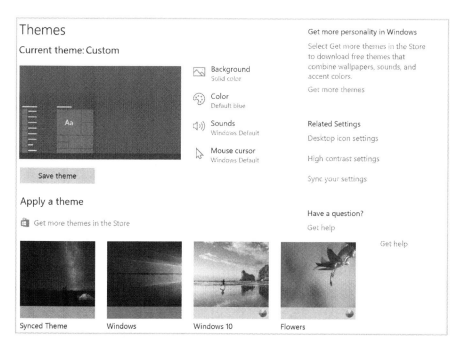

Windows 10 provides three default themes for normal usage – just click one to activate it. It is also possible to alter the default themes and to create your own. To do the latter, just activate one of the default themes and then make the changes you want to it, i.e. the Desktop and Lock screen backgrounds, the computer's sound effects, the mouse pointer, icon size – there are many things you can customise.

When you have things just as you want them, go back to the Personalization screen and click **Save Theme.** Give your new theme a name and then click the **Save** button. It can now be selected or deselected at any time.

Adjust and Alter Your Computer's Sounds

Some computers have a volume control, some don't. If yours doesn't, you can use the one supplied by Windows 10. Type **volume** into the Taskbar search box and press **Enter** to open the system volume control. This lets you adjust the volume of the computer's speakers, plus the volume of system sounds – those jingles and clicks you hear from time to time.

Now open the Control Panel and click **Sound**. Then click the **Sounds** tab. The drop-down box under **Sound Scheme** lets you select from the sound schemes installed on the computer.

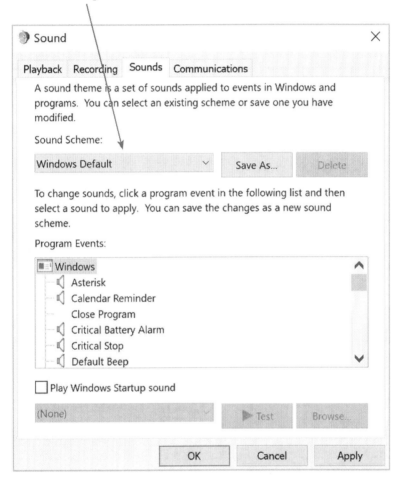

Under **Program Events,** you will see a list of all the Windows clicks and jingles and the events that generate them. Click any of these events and then apply a different sound to it from the drop-down box under **Sounds** at the bottom.

You can preview all the sounds by clicking the **Test** button. Finally, click the **Apply** button.

Changing and Resizing Icons and Tiles

Like just about everything else in Windows, even the Desktop icons and Start menu tiles can be customised.

Desktop Icons

To change the size of the Desktop icons, right-click on the Desktop and, from the menu, select **View**.

You'll see three size options: Small, Medium and Large. Make your choice and it will be applied immediately.

Should you want to, you can remove all the icons from the Desktop by unchecking **Show desktop icons**. You can also change some of the system Desktop icons. To do this, open the Personalization screen and click **Themes**. Under **Related Settings**, click **Desktop Icon Settings** to open this window

Click one of the icons in the main window and then click **Change Icon**. A window will open with a list of dozens of alternative icons that you can use. Just select one and click **OK**.

At the top of the window, checking and unchecking the boxes will add or remove the associated icons from the desktop.

Tiles

It is also possible to change the size of the Start menu tiles. To do this, right-click on the tile and then click **Resize** to open the menu shown below:

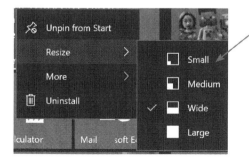

Select from the options offered: Small, Medium, Wide and Large.

The Wide option will double the width of the tile, while the Large option will double it in both width and height.

Associate a Picture With Your Account

By default, Windows 10 assigns a generic silhouette for the user's account picture. You can change this by opening the Start menu and clicking the account button at the bottom-left. Then click **Change account settings.**

Under Create your picture, click the **Browse for one** button to open your pictures folder. Select one and then click the **Choose picture** button.

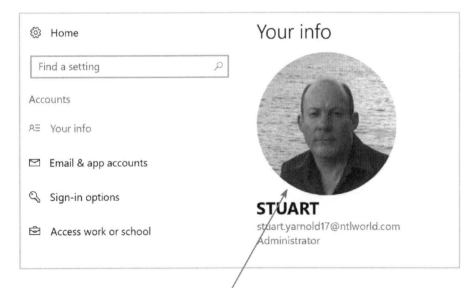

The selected picture will now be assigned to your account.

Add, Move and Resize Tiles on the Start Menu

Out of the box, many people are going to find the Start menu is not to their taste. Fortunately, just about every aspect of it can be changed as we see below.

Moving Tiles

One of the first things you will want to do is change the position of some or all of the default tiles. This is very simple – left-click on the tile and drag it to where you want it to go – when in position, release it. You can also drag tiles to the Desktop; in this case, though, the tile is not moved, just copied. Below, we see the Calendar and Weather apps copied to the author's Desktop.

Removing Tiles

It's almost a certainty that you will find many of the default tiles superfluous to your requirements and that the space they occupy can be put to better use. To remove a tile from the Start menu, right-click on it. A menu will open showing several options: Select the top option, **Unpin from Start**. Note that this does not delete the tile's app from the PC, it just removes it from the Start menu.

Adding Tiles

Now that you've created some space on the Start menu, it's time to put something on it that you're going to use. You can use the search box on the Taskbar, the Control Panel or the list of apps on the Start menu to locate the required apps and programs. Having found one click on it and drag it to the menu. Note that you can only add tiles – system folders can't be added.

Change Screen Resolution

The resolution of your monitor screen affects the size of the items it displays. If it is set too high, it could well be that icons and text will be too small to be read comfortably, and vice versa. Set it to your liking as follows:

1. Right-click on the Desktop and then click **Display settings.** The Display Settings window will open

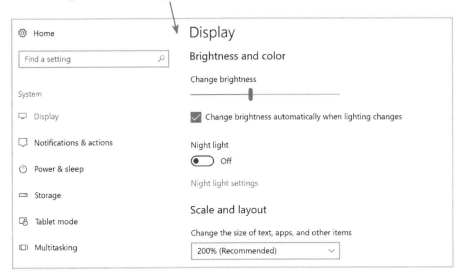

2. By default, Windows sets the resolution to what it considers to be the optimum setting. However, if you wish to try a different setting open the drop-down menu under **Resolution.**

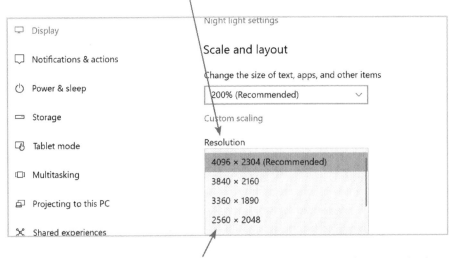

3. The resolutions your monitor is capable of displaying are shown in the list. Select one and then click **Keep changes**

Improve Display Quality With ClearType

ClearType font technology delivers improved font display quality over traditional forms of font smoothing or anti-aliasing. ClearType improves readability on colour LCD displays with a digital interface, such as those in laptops and high-quality flat panel displays.

It's on by default in Windows 10 but you can fine-tune the settings as we explain below:

1. Type **cleartype** into the Taskbar search box and press **Enter**

2. At the opening screen, click **Next**

3. At the second screen, Windows checks that you are using the correct (native) resolution for your monitor. Click **Next**

4. There then follows a series of screens showing different samples of text

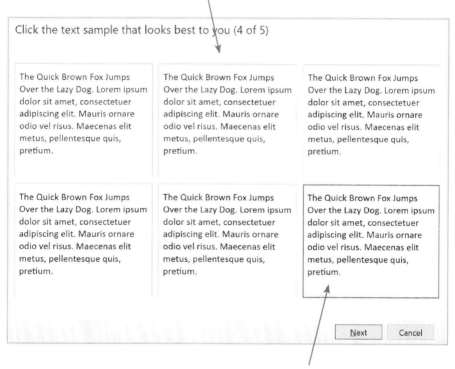

5. Select the sample that looks best to you by clicking on it and then click **Next** at the bottom. At the final screen, click **Finish** to exit the ClearType tuner – your selection will now be applied

While not for everybody, many people find that ClearType improves the legibility of screen text considerably.

Accessibility Options For the Disabled

Many people have disabilities that make it difficult to use a computer. For these users, Windows 10 provides a range of accessibility options that can make a big difference to their use of the computer.

Discover what options are available by typing **ease** in to the Taskbar search box and pressing **Enter**. The **Ease of Access Center** opens:

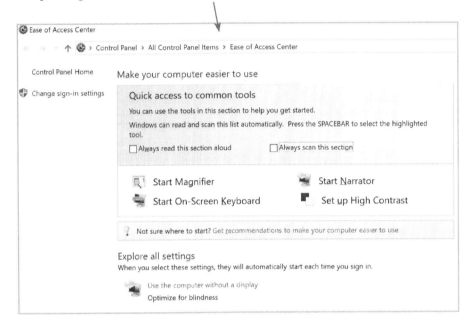

You will see many options here so if you're a bit confused we suggest you click the yellow **Not sure where to start?** box. This opens a question and answer screen that gives Windows some information regarding your disabilities. It will then make recommendations based on the information you have provided.

Alternatively, right at the top of the screen, you'll see some commonly used accessibility tools. These include:

- **Magnifier** – when activated, Magnifier will run when you log on to your computer. Magnifier enlarges the part of the screen where the mouse is pointing and can be particularly useful for viewing objects that are difficult to see

- **Narrator** – Narrator reads aloud on-screen text and describes events (such as error messages appearing) that happen while you're using the computer

- **On-Screen Keyboard** – the on-screen keyboard displays a visual keyboard with all the standard keys. You can select keys using the mouse or another pointing device, and you can use a single key, or group of keys, to cycle through the keys on the screen

- **High Contrast** – this option lets you set a high-contrast colour scheme that heightens the colour contrast of some text and images on your computer screen, thus making those items more distinct and easier to identify

Moving down the screen, you'll see some more accessibility options. These include:

- **Use the computer without a display** – clicking this opens a screen that offers a range of accessibility aids designed to help the blind. These include Narrator and Audio description

- **Make the computer easier to see** – this is for those whose eyesight is poor. Options include High contrast colour scheme, Narrator, Audio description, Magnifier, thickness of the blinking cursor and more

- **Use the computer without a mouse or keyboard** – for people who cannot use a physical keyboard, this screen offers options for activating an on-screen keyboard and using speech recognition

- **Make the mouse easier to use** – this screen provides options for changing the colour and size of the mouse pointer, using mouse keys (controlling the mouse with the numeric keypad) and activating windows by mouse hover

- **Make the keyboard easier to use** – options on this screen include turning on Sticky keys, Mouse keys, Toggle keys and Filter keys

- **Use text or visual alternatives for sounds** – for people who are deaf options here provide visual cues to replace sounds. These include flashing active captions bars, flashing active window and flashing desktop

- **Make it easier to focus on tasks** – options here help to reduce the amount of information on your screen so that it's easier to read. Aids include Narrator, Sticky keys, Toggle keys and turning off unnecessary animations

- **Make touch and tablets easier to use** – this option lets you specify an accessibility tool to be launched when the Windows and volume buttons are pressed simultaneously

Be On Time With Windows 10

For those of you who like to be on time, Windows 10 offers a Date and Time utility that can be accessed in the Control Panel.

The utility opens on the Date and Time tab, which gives you options to change the date and the time, and to change the time zone.

The Additional Clocks tab lets you create additional clocks to display the time in other time zones. These can be viewed by clicking on or hovering the mouse over the Taskbar clock.

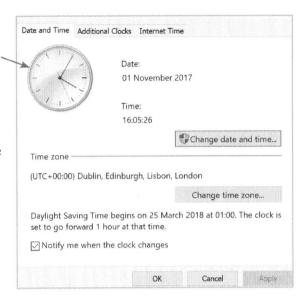

The Internet Time tab lets you synchronise your computer with a number of Internet time servers to make sure it is dead on time. Select a time server from the Server drop-down box and then click the **Update now** button.

Windows 10 also offers a Time & Language app. To access this go to **Start menu > Settings > Time & Language**. The app opens in the Date & Time view as we see below:

The Time & Language app offers much the same options as the Control Panel's Date and Time utility.

CHAPTER 7

Managing Your Hardware

Computer hardware includes printers, scanners, cameras, external drives, flash drives, network adapters and modems to name just some.

These devices need to be installed – this involves physically connecting them to the computer, getting the computer to recognis e them and then setting them up as per your requirements.

Modern computers make this process much easier than it used to be but issues can still occur. In this chapter, we explain all you need to know.

Where to Find Your Devices

To help you keep an eye on what hardware is installed on your computer, Windows provides several utilities. Two of these are:

Device Manager

The Device Manager can be accessed from the Control Panel. When opened, it shows a categorised list of all the hardware installed on the computer.

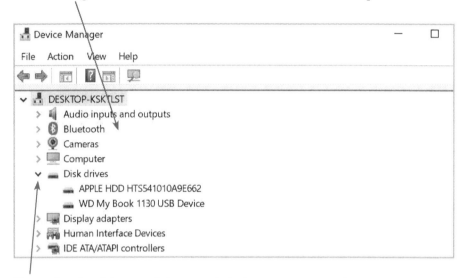

To see details of the actual devices, click the arrow next to them.

Devices and Printers

This utility can also be accessed from the Control Panel. When it opens, it shows all the devices on your PC as we see below. These include printers, the mouse, external hard drives and keyboards, etc.

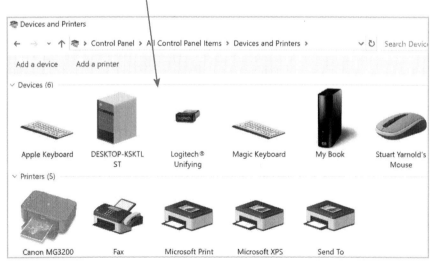

How to Install a Device

We mentioned in the introduction to this chapter that modern PCs are much better at installing hardware devices than they used to be, and indeed they are.

Usually, all that's required is that you connect the device to the appropriate port on the computer and then switch it on. Windows will search its built-in driver database for the device's driver (see page 103) and, assuming it has it, will install it automatically. The device should then be ready for operation.

However, things don't always go to plan, in which case you will have to do it the hard way as we describe below:

1. Click the **Start** button and then click **Settings**

2. Click **Devices**

3. The Devices window opens – on the left, you'll see a generic list of devices that can be installed on the computer. Click the one that's relevant

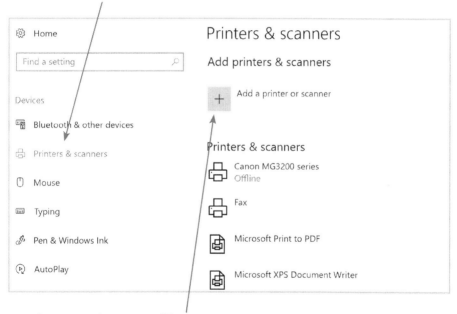

4. A new window opens. Using a printer as an example, click the **Add a printer or scanner** button- Windows will now do a search for recently added printing devices and show a list of any it has found

5. If your device is in the list, click it and then follow the prompts – this will install the device and also usually fix any problems with the device

6. Again, using a printer as an example, if your printer isn't in the list, click the **The printer that I want isn't listed** link at the top of the screen

cont'd

7. A Help page will open offering advice on how to resolve the issue

If your device comes with an installation disc (unlikely these days, it must be said), this gives you another option. The procedure for this is:

1. Place the installation disc in the CD/DVD drive

2. Open This PC and click on the CD/DVD drive to open the disc

3. A User Account Control box will open asking permission to proceed – click Yes

4. The device's installation screen will now open. An example is shown below:

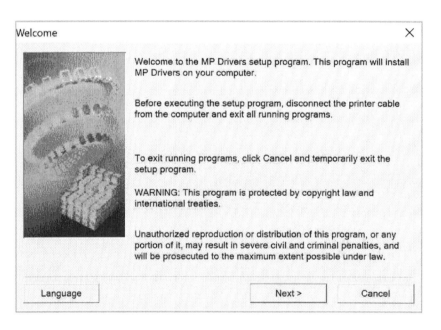

5. Installation options vary according to the device but it's usually just a matter of following the prompts and clicking **Next**

Keep Your Devices Updated

We mentioned device drivers on page 101 – virtually all devices are supplied with one. Drivers are small programs that basically tell the computer what system resources the device requires in order to function properly. There are device drivers for printers, monitors, disk drives and so on. Having installed a device successfully, many people then basically forget all it – as long as it works, that's all they are concerned about.

However, nothing stays still in the world of computing for long. A few months after marketing a device, the device's manufacturer may add new features to it that the original driver can't support. To be able to use the new features, you will need to update the driver. Drivers can also become corrupted so that the device doesn't work properly any more. This will require the driver to be reinstalled. However if an updated version is available, it makes sense to install that instead.

Most devices these days are capable of updating themselves – as soon as the manufacturer makes an update available, they will download and install it automatically (as long as the computer is connected to the Internet). Not all devices update themselves automatically though, so there may be times when you will have to do it manually.

Updating a Device Driver
If you have a device connected to your system that you think may benefit from a driver update, this is the way to go about it:

1. Go to the Control Panel and open Device Manager

2. Locate the device to be updated and right-click on it

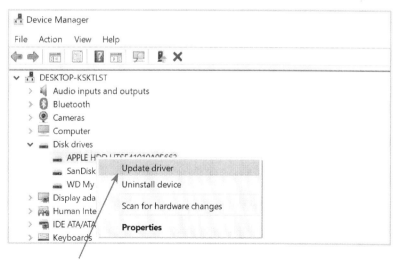

3. Click **Update Driver**

cont'd

4. A window will open asking how you want to search for the driver

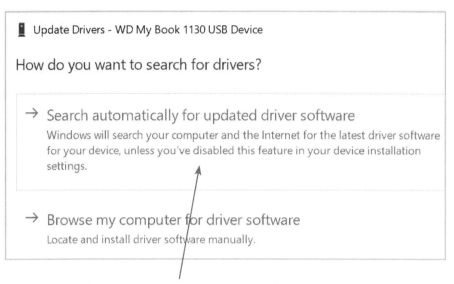

5. Click the first option, **Search automatically for updated driver software.**

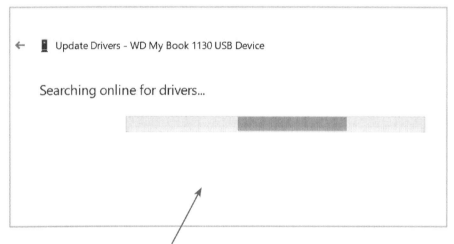

6. Windows will now perform a search of both the Internet and your computer for a more recent driver. If it finds one, it will install it automatically; if it doesn't, you will get a message saying that you already have the best driver installed

How to Uninstall a Device

All devices eventually outlive their usefulness; at this point they can be removed from the system, i.e. uninstalled. There are two ways to do this – the correct way and the incorrect way.

The incorrect way is to just disconnect it from the computer and assume the job's done. This can give rise to two problems:

• Windows will think the device is still installed but has a problem. As a result, you may get unwanted and unnecessary error messages

• The device's configuration details will still be held by Windows. Should you later replace the device with a more modern version, or a similar one from a different manufacturer, the original configuration settings may cause problems with the new device

The correct way is to uninstall it in Windows before you disconnect it from the computer.

The procedure is:

1. Go to the Control Panel and open Device Manager

2. Locate the device to be uninstalled and right-click on it

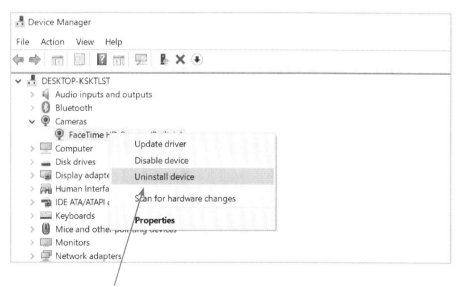

3. In the flyout menu, click **Uninstall device**

Windows will delete all traces of the device's configuration details. Now you can safely disconnect it from your computer.

Connecting Bluetooth Devices

Bluetooth is a short-range wireless network technology that makes it possible to use a variety of wireless devices with your PC – Bluetooth headphones, speakers, phones, fitness trackers – to name just a few.

Establishing a Bluetooth Connection

Before you can use a Bluetooth device, it must first be paired with your computer, i.e. they need to be 'introduced' so that they are on the same wavelength so to speak. To do it:

1. Switch on your Bluetooth device and make it discoverable. The procedure for doing this will be in the device's documentation

2. Turn on Bluetooth on your PC, if it's not already. To do this, go to **Start** > **Settings** > **Devices**. Click **Bluetooth & other devices** at the left

3. Make sure Bluetooth is on

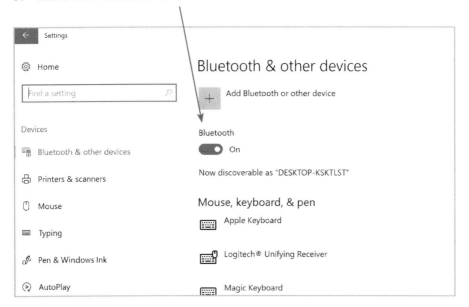

4. Windows will now do a search for nearby Bluetooth devices and connect to any it finds

If Windows doesn't find your device, the following may resolve the issue:

*   Make sure your device actually supports Bluetooth

*   Try updating the device's driver as explained on pages 103-104

*   Check that the device is switched on and has been made discoverable. Consult the device's documentation to make sure you are doing it correctly

CHAPTER 8

The Internet

Windows 10 introduces a new web browser. This is called Edge and it replaces the aging Internet Explorer.

Edge has been designed to be lightweight with a layout engine built around current web standards. It removes support for legacy technologies such as ActiveX in favor of extensions and integration with other Microsoft services, such as the digital assistant Cortana, and OneDrive.

Introducing the Edge Web Browser

For two decades, the default web browser in Windows has been Internet Explorer. Over the years, the browser has become bloated, insecure and confusing to use.

For these reasons, a lot of people are using alternatives such as Google Chrome and Mozilla Firefox. With Windows 10, Microsoft has gone back to the drawing board and scrapped everything it had done so far with Internet Explorer. It has come up with an entirely new browser from scratch, one that is intended to shed all of the baggage of Internet Explorer and so offer a modern, fast web browsing experience for Windows users. Edge has been built to be clean, tight and responsive.

Internet Explorer is still alive – just – and is also supplied with Windows 10. However, it's buried away in the operating system and Microsoft says that's largely for compatibility with legacy enterprise apps.

Edge is the default browser and it is available across Microsoft's product line, from computers to smartphones to Holo Lens and Surface Hub.

One of the new browser's coolest features is integration with Cortana, which pops up here and there as you browse with Edge, providing context when you highlight a word and choose **Ask Cortana**, or when you type in queries for weather and other common search terms in Edge's search box.

Edge has other new features. A Reading list lets you save articles and web pages for later reading, though it doesn't work offline. Edge can also present a page in a stripped-down format that removes ads and extraneous banners for easier reading, similar to Apple's Safari browser on OS X. A note-taking mode lets you doodle on and mark up a web page, then save it as an image to OneNote or share it with another app.

However, it doesn't have a number of the power features that Chrome and Firefox users have long been accustomed to.

As it stands, Edge is not quite as good or feature-complete as it could be. That said, it's already much better than Internet Explorer.

The Main Elements of Edge

The first thing you notice when you open Edge is it's simple, uncluttered and clean design. Lets take a look at the browser's main elements:

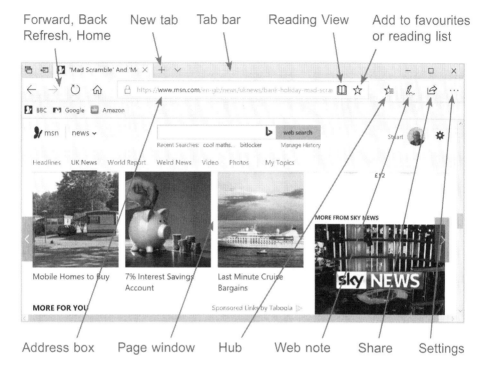

Forward, Back Refresh, Home | New tab | Tab bar | Reading View | Add to favourites or reading list

Address box | Page window | Hub | Web note | Share | Settings

Edge's Octane 2 speed performance in comparison to Google's Chrome and Mozilla's Firefox. Octane 2 is a benchmark test of a web browser's performance.

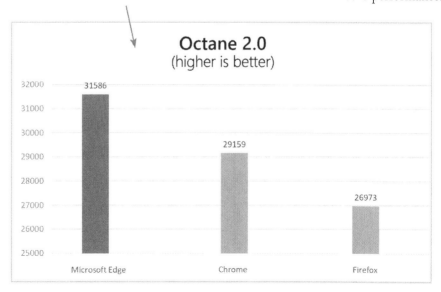

Setting a Home Page

When you open Edge, by default, it opens at a page of its own choosing. Few users are going to put up with this, so below we explain how to configure Edge to open at a page determined by you.

1. Click the **Settings and more** button at the top-right of the browser

2. Click **Settings** at the bottom of the menu

3. The **Start page** option is selected by default

4. Deselect the **Start page** option by clicking **A specific page or pages**

5. In the **Enter a URL** box that opens below, enter the website that you want Edge to open when you start it up

6. Finish by clicking on the **Save** button

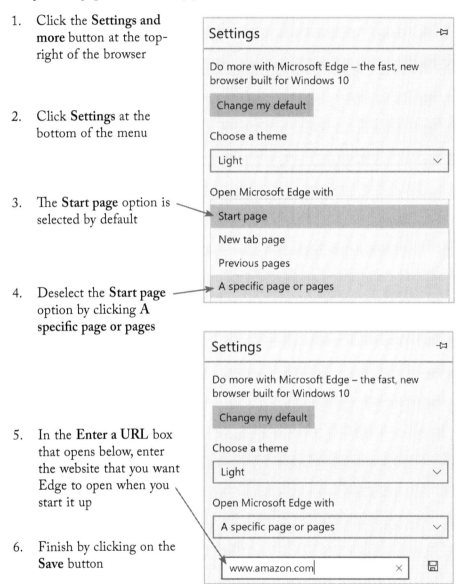

From now on, every time you start Edge, it will open at the web page you have specified at Step 5.

Opening a Web Page

To open a web page with Edge, you first have to enter an address. This is done with the browser's 'smart address bar' (these are now common in modern browsers).

They are called 'smart' because they offer more than just one function. The address bar in Edge lets you enter the required address, open the page at the address and can also be used as a search box.

To use the address bar, just start typing the address of the site you want to visit – as you do so, a list appears below showing both suggested web sites and search suggestions – this is the bar carrying out two functions at the same time.

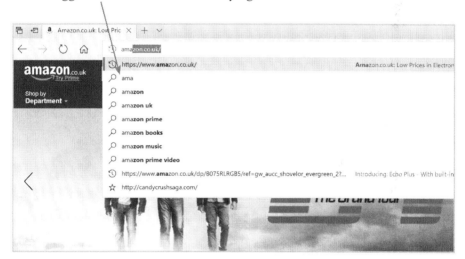

If one of the suggestions is what you are looking for, click on it to go the page.

You can also use Cortana to open web pages. Just speak the web site's address into your microphone and Edge will open the site.

Tab Browsing

Tabbed browsing is a feature found on all modern web browsers. It lets you have a number of web pages open at the same time and quickly switch between them by clicking the appropriate tab.

1. Open Edge

2. Right at the top of the browser is the Tab bar

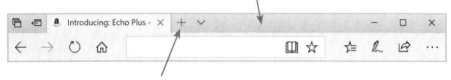

3. Click the + button on the Tab bar to open a tab

4. In the new tab, enter the address of the required web page in the address box or click one of the **Top sites** listed in the main window

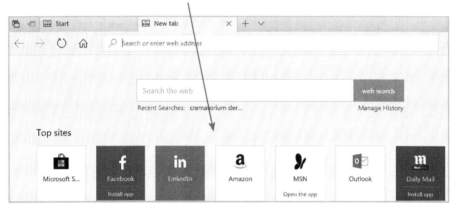

5. As you open more tabs, they are added to the Tab bar. Each open tab is named after the site open in it – this lets you distinguish between them

6. To open a tab, just click on it

Some useful tab features include being able to rearrange tabs on the bar by dragging them left and right. Right-clicking on an element in a page reveals an option to open that element in a new tab. Also, you can change the default Start page when a tab is opened – you'll find this option in Edge's settings.

Quickly Access Your Favourite Websites

Everyone who uses the Internet has sites they visit more often than others. You can save yourself the bother of having to type the address of these sites each time you want to visit them by making use of Edge's Favourites feature.

Creating Favourites

With the site open, click the **Add to favourites or reading list** button. Then click **Favourites**.

The page's name is entered in the Name box – change it if you want to.

By default, the favourite is created in the Favourites folder. By clicking the down-arrow and then **Create new folder** below, you can create your own Favourites folder. This can be useful when you have a lot of favourites and they need to be organised.

When you're ready to save the favourite, click the **Add** button.

Opening Favourites

Having created a favourite, you now need some way of accessing it. Look at Edge's interface and you'll see no obvious way to do it. The solution is twofold:

The first is via Edge's Hub feature - we explain how to do this on page 117. The second is to open a Favourites bar that sits just under the Address bar and provides instant access. Do this as follows:

Click the **Settings and more** button at the top-right of the browser and then click **Settings**. Click **Show the favourites bar** to **On**. The empty Favourites bar will appear under the address bar.

You now have to move the existing favourites to the Favourites bar. Do this by going to **Settings and more > Favourites**. You'll see a Favourites Bar folder at the top followed by your list of favourites. Simply left-click on each one and drag it to the Favourites Bar folder. You will now be able to see them on the Favourites Bar.

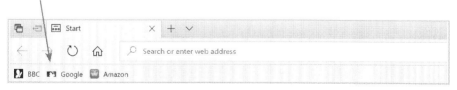

Save Articles For Later With Reading Lists

The Reading list feature in Edge provides you with a place to save articles or other content that you want to read later – on the bus, over the weekend – wherever and whenever you like. As the content is saved on your computer, an Internet connection is not required to read it.

To save an article in your reading list:

1. Open the web page that you want to add to it

2. Click the **Add to favourites or reading list** button on the toolbar

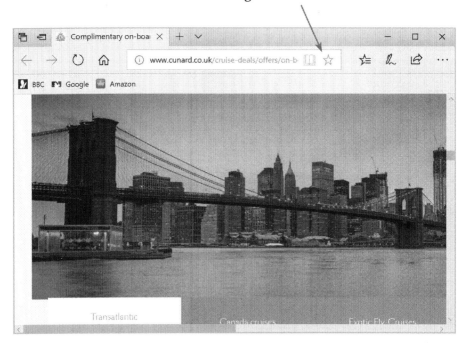

3. Click **Reading list**. If you want to, you can rename the link in the Name box provided. Then click the **Add** button

4. Saved articles can be opened later on via Edge's Hub feature as we explain on page 117

As it stands, the Reading list feature is rather basic as you can only save links to it. You do not have the option to create folders, or to auto-delete items after a specified number of days.

Eliminate Screen Clutter With Reading View

On many web pages these days, it is difficult to find the content – the reason you opened the page in the first place – due to the proliferation of extraneous web objects such as video clips, images, ads and banners. Sometimes, the content can be enhanced by it but, more often than not, it is just a pain.

The Reading view feature provided by Edge solves this problem by stripping out all content other than the article itself. To use it, open the web page containing the article that you want to read. It will probably be loaded with ads and other rubbish like the one shown below.

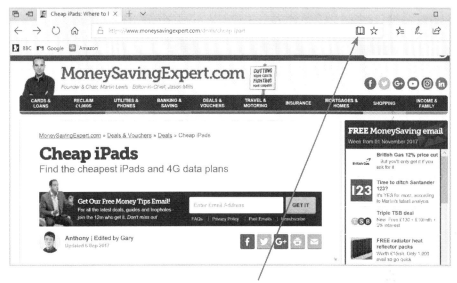

Click the **Reading view** button at the right of the address bar

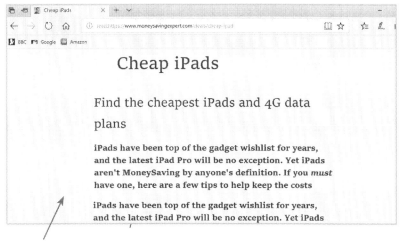

Read the article in peace and quite with no ads, etc, to distract you

Take Web Notes With Edge's Notes Utility

Edge lets you write, doodle and highlight directly on web pages as a note. Afterwards, you can save or share the web note. To use the Notes feature:

1. Open the web page and click the **Add Notes** button

2. The toolbar and tab will turn purple in colour, indicating that you are currently viewing or making a web note on the page. At the top-right of the browser, you will see eight buttons. From left to right, these are: Ballpoint pen, Highlighter, Eraser, Add a note, Clip, Touch writing, Save Web Note and Share Web Note

3. Click the **Ballpoint Pen** button once to open the pen. Double-click to open a menu from where you can select the pen size and the ink colour

4. Click the **Add a Note** button and then click on the page. A note window will open as we see below:

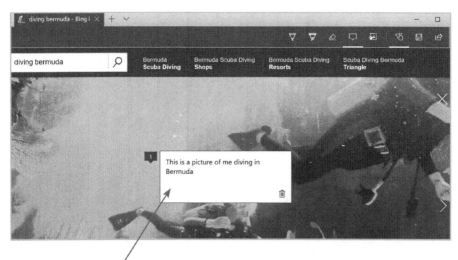

5. Write your note

6. Another option is provided by the **Clip** tool. Click the **Clip** button and then you will be able to draw a rectangle around any part of the screen you want to save as a note

7. Having written your note or clip, you now need to click the **Save Web Note** button at the right of the purple toolbar. Save options include sending it to OneNote or saving in Edge's Favourites or Reading list

Find it Quickly in the Hub

The Hub is a central location within Edge that is used to store a number of different things. It enables you to find them quickly and works as follows:

1. On Edge's toolbar, click the **Hub** button

2. A sidebar will open with four buttons at the top. From left to right, these are: Favourites, Reading List, History and Downloads

Favourites
We described how the Favourites feature in Edge works on page 113. Saved favourites can be viewed via the Favourites bar that can be placed on the browser window, and also in the Hub. Just open the Hub and click the **Favourites** button.

Reading list
We described how to add content to the Reading list on page 114. In order to access and read that content, you need to open the Hub and click the **Reading list** button. It shows a chronological list of all the content you have saved for later reading. Having read an article, you can delete it by right-clicking and clicking **Delete**.

History
Click the **History** button for a detailed history of your web browsing activities. Details of every site you have visited, plus the date and time, are all recorded and available for viewing from the list. You can delete the entire list by clicking the **Clear history** link at the top-right and individual entries via the right-click menu.

Downloads
The Downloads button opens a list of everything you have downloaded to your computer. That's it really – you have no options here other than to see what has been downloaded.

As a final note, you can pin any of the above in a permanently open view by clicking the **Pin** icon at the top-right.

Surf Safely With InPrivate Browsing

Online security is a very important issue these days, and in more ways than one. Yes, we all want to keep hackers out of our bank accounts and big corporations from snooping through our emails. But there's also the issue of browsing the Internet – how can we keep this private?

The answer to this comes in the form of Edge's InPrivate browsing feature. To get going with this:

1. Open the browser

2. Click the **Settings and more** button at the far-right of the toolbar

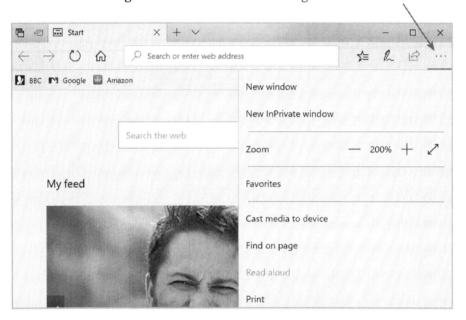

3. Click **New InPrivate window**

4. A new browser window will open. It will look and act exactly the same as a regular browser window does. The only indication you will have that you are in InPrivate mode is the blue **InPrivate** label at the top-left of the browser window

When you exit InPrivate mode, all the data that Edge has collected during the session is deleted from the computer. Information that is discarded includes cookies, temporary internet files, web page history, form data and passwords, and the anti-phishing cache to mention just some.

As a result, you are able to surf the web without leaving an electronic trail that anyone with the requisite knowledge and tools can follow.

Pin Websites to the Start Menu and Taskbar

A cool feature available in Edge is 'Pinning'. This lets you pin a web page to both the Start menu and Taskbar. Once done, you can then go to the page immediately without having to start up Edge first. Do it as follows:

1. Open Edge and go to the page you want to pin

2. Click the **Settings and more** button and then click either **Pin this page to Start** or **Pin this page to the taskbar**

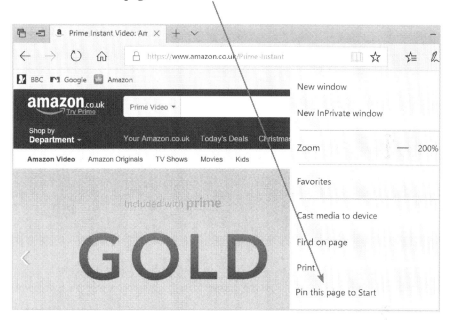

3. Close Edge and go to the Start menu on the computer. Look in the tile section at the right and you will find a tile that shows the web site's logo

4. Click the tile and Edge will open the page in a new browser. As it's a live tile, it may display real-time information that is regularly updated

Select Text Precisely With Caret Browsing

When selecting text in a web page, it can be difficult to select precisely what you want without also selecting adjacent text, and objects such as images and tables, as we see in the example below. Caret browsing can help with this issue.

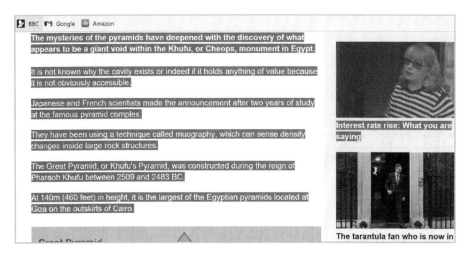

Functionality
When caret browsing is enabled, click anywhere on the page to place a caret - also known as a text cursor - in that location. You can then use various keys on your keyboard, including Home, End, Page Up, Page Down and the arrow keys to move the caret around the page. To select text, hold the Shift key and move the caret; you can then copy it with the usual Ctrl-C keyboard shortcut.

Opening Links
When the caret reaches a link, the link becomes active and is highlighted with a dotted border. Tap **Enter** to open it in the same tab, **Shift-Enter** to open it in a new window, **Ctrl-Enter** to open it in a new background tab and **Ctrl-Shift-Enter** to open it in a new foreground tab. Alternatively, since enabling caret browsing doesn't deactivate the mouse, you can open links using your mouse as usual.

Enabling & Disabling Caret Browsing
In previous versions of Edge, there was a setting in the Advanced Settings page that allowed caret browsing to be turned on and off. For some reason, that's gone now. In the latest incarnation of Edge, you need to prss the F7 key to activate caret browsing. In the confirmation window that appears, click **Turn on**.

To disable caret browsing, press the **F7** key again and click **Yes** in the confirmation window.

Specify the Search Engine to Use With Edge

By default, all searches conducted with the Edge browser will be done with Microsoft's Bing search engine. If you are happy with this, fine. If not, you can specify your own choice of search provider.

To do it:

1. Click the **Settings and more** button

2. In the window that opens click **Settings** at the bottom

3. Scroll down and click **View advanced settings**

4. Under **Search in the address bar with Bing**, click the **Change search engine** box

5. In the window that opens you will see a list of search providers that vary according to the websites you have visited

6. Select the one you want

7. Click **Set as default**. From this point on, all searches will be done with the selected search provider

However, if the desired search provider isn't in the list, do the following:

Browse to the website of the desired search provider. Click **Settings and more** on the toolbar, **Settings** and then **View advanced settings**. Then click **Change search engine**.

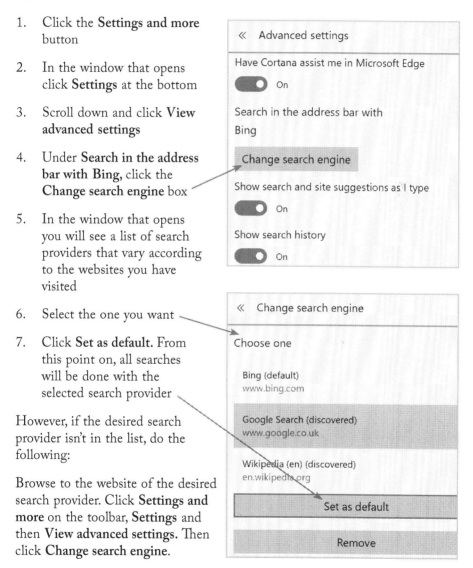

You will see that the search engine you have open in your browser is now in the list of available search engines. Select it and then click **Set as default**.

Browser Settings

We've highlighted some of the many settings available for the Edge browser in this chapter. To see what other settings are available, click the **Settings and more** button at the top far-right of the browser and then click **Settings**.

Appearance
Just one option is available here – **Choose a theme** – you can choose between Light and Dark. Both of these will be useful for users whose eyesight is perhaps not quite as good as they'd like.

Block Pop-ups
Click Advanced Settings. Pop-ups are advertisement windows that appear as you browse through a web page. They are usually a complete pain in the ass and having them automatically blocked is perhaps not a bad thing. You may, however, prefer to make your own mind up about this rather than having Microsoft do it for you – if so, you can disable the automatic blocking by clicking the Block pop-ups switch to **Off.**

Privacy and services
There are two options here, both enabled by default, that you ought to consider. The **Offer to save passwords** and **Save form entries** options are potential security risks as another person who uses the computer will be able to access your password-protected pages, and to auto-fill various types of online forms.

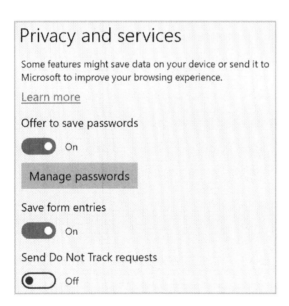

It depends what you use your computer for but our recommendation is that you disable both of these options by clicking them to **Off.**

CHAPTER 9

Setting Up and Using Email

In Chapter 9 we look at how you can use your computer to communicate with the world outside via email. We show you everything you need to know in this respect – types of email account, how to set up an email account and how to use the email app supplied with Windows 10.

A related application is People, which provides you with a digital address book – we explain how to use this to the best effect.

What is Email?

Short for electronic mail, email is the transmission of text messages over communications networks. All email programs include a text editor for composing the messages and basic formatting tools that include bold, italics, font and font colour.

All users have their own unique email address which the sender uses to address the email. It is possible to send the same message to several users at once.

Sent messages are stored in electronic mailboxes (called the Inbox in email programs) until the recipient opens them. To see if you have any email, you need to check your inbox periodically, although most email programs alert you when email is received. After reading your email, you can store it, forward it to other users or delete it. They can also be printed if you want a hard copy.

All online services and Internet Service Providers (ISPs) offer email, and most also support gateways so that you can exchange email with users of other systems. Usually, it takes only a few seconds or minutes for email to arrive at its destination.

There are two ways to use email. The first is via web mail which, as the name suggests, is done online. The second is with an email program which is installed on the user's computer

Web Mail
With web mail, messages are sent and received via a web browser. There are a number of web mail providers, such as Gmail, Outlook.com and Yahoo Mail. These services are free and all you have to do to use one is to open an account with the provider.

You will then be able to send and receive email, not just from your own computer, but from any computer as long as it is connected to the Internet. For example, at a friends house, a public library or a wireless hotspot.

Email Programs
There are many different email programs, all of which do essentially the same thing. The only difference between them is the number of features provided. As these programs are installed on the user's computer and can be used from there, it is not necessary to go online to send and receive messages as with web mail.

While email programs usually provide more features than web mail, one disadvantage is that email can only be used with the computer that has the email program installed on it. You are also more likely to lose emails through accidental deletion and problems with your computer than you are with web mail where the messages are all safely stored online.

Windows 10's Mail App

Windows 8 featured a very basic app for email, which was improved in 8.1 with things like drag-and-drop for moving mail among folders. The Windows 10 Mail app that replaces it is actually part of the free version of Microsoft's Office Mobile productivity suite.

It's called Outlook Mail on Windows 10 Mobile that runs on smartphones and tablets, but just plain Mail on Windows 10 for computers. The email app comes with touch support and a new minimalist flat design and is a big advance over the Windows 8.1 Mail app.

If you need to set up an email account, the Mail app supports all the standard mail systems, including Outlook.com, Exchange, Gmail, Yahoo! Mail, iCloud, and any POP or IMAP account you may have.

Simply enter your address and password for any of the account types and Mail will figure out the required server settings. A big advantage of using Mail instead of web mail is that new messages will appear above the Notification area at the bottom-right corner of the Desktop.

Mail's interface is minimalist and clean, and gets out of the way so you can concentrate on your emails. While it is designed for touch, using it with a keyboard and mouse is completely natural and fluid. It's a clear interface that works well in either setting.

The ability to connect multiple accounts, and fluid formatting and insertion choices, mean it's up to all but the most demanding email tasks. The integration with Notifications is another plus for the app, as is the fact that once you set it up on one Windows 10 device, any others you sign into will require no email setup whatsoever.

Email Services and Protocols

Before you can use the Mail app, you must first set up an email account or add an existing one to it. This is very easy to do – if you currently use one of the popular email services such as iCloud, Gmail, Yahoo, etc, it's even easier as much of the work is already done for you – a few clicks are all that's needed.

If you decide to use a different service though, such as the one from your ISP, you will need to provide more information. Most email services are web-based and use the IMAP protocol (except for Microsoft Exchange, which uses the MAPI protocol).

The Mail app in Windows 10 knows how to connect to all these services – all you need to supply is the email address and account password. If, however, you don't use any of these services, you will have to supply more information.

Apart from the email address and account password, you will also need to provide the names of the incoming and outgoing mail servers, plus any security information required to send email. You will also need to specify if the account is POP or IMAP.

All this information will be available from your email service provider – just ask them for it and you'll be ready to go. However, before we go into the mechanics of setting up an email account, we'll explain the difference between the email protocols POP and IMAP.

- **POP (Post Office Protocol)** – with POP, emails are stored temporarily on your Internet Service Provider's (ISP's) server. When you connect to the server, the messages are downloaded to your computer and then deleted from the server

  The advantage of POP is that because all your emails are stored on the computer, they can be re-read at any time without the need to reconnect to the server. The disadvantage is that they can only be viewed on the computer to which they were downloaded

- **IMAP (Internet Message Access Protocol)** – IMAP essentially works the other way. Messages are not downloaded to your computer (although it may seem as though they are). They are actually stored permanently on the ISP's server and you simply read them from there

  The advantage with this method is that your email can be accessed via any device regardless of its location. The disadvantage is that in order to do so, an Internet connection is necessary

How to Set Up an Email Account

When you come to set up an email account, you can either use an existing one or create a new one from scratch. We'll see how to set up the former as most people these days already have an account.

1. Open the Start menu and click the **Mail** app. On the sidebar at the left, click **Accounts**. Then click **Manage Accounts** at the top-right

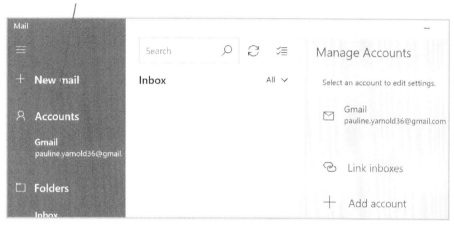

2. Click **Add account**

3. In the **Choose an account** window, select who your account is with – Google, Yahoo, etc. If none of them apply, click the **Other account** option

4. A sign-in window will open – just enter your email address and password in the boxes provided. Then click the **Sign-in** button

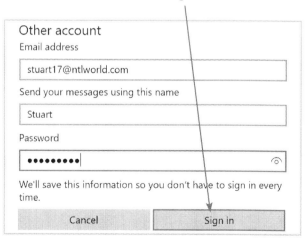

5. Assuming your details check out, your email account is set up with Mail without further ado – you're good to go

Receiving and Storing Email

With your email account set up, incoming messages will be received by the Mail app. The number of unread emails is indicated by the number at the right of the Inbox.

Email folders   Selected email   Message window

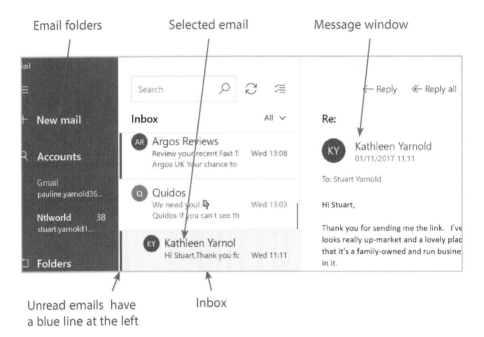

Unread emails have   Inbox
a blue line at the left

When you click the Mail app on the Start menu, it will open as shown above. Your email folders are in the side bar at the left, the Inbox is in the middle and the message window is at the right.

To read a message, just click on it in the Inbox and it will open in the message window at the right of the screen.

Unread emails are indicated by a dark blue vertical bar at the left of the email in the Inbox.

To see all messages that haven't been read yet, click the **All** button at the top of the Inbox and then click **Unread** from the menu. Having caught up with your emails, click **Unread** and then click **All** to return to the normal Inbox view

To check for new email, click the **Sync this view** button at the top of the Inbox. When the check is complete, you will see an **Up to date** message at the bottom of the Inbox.

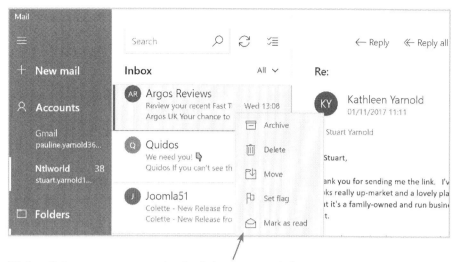

Right-click on any message in the Inbox to reveal these options:

- **Archive** – archiving a message removes it from the Inbox but doesn't delete it – you can access it whenever you need to

- **Delete** – removes the email from the Mail app

- **Move** – this option opens a list of all the email folders in the account. Choose one to move the email to

- **Set Flag** – flags the email in the Inbox by turning it yellow

- **Mark as unread** – places a dark blue horizontal bar at the front of the email to indicate it hasn't been read yet

- **Move to Spam**– this moves a message to the Spam folder. Future messages from the sender will be automatically moved to the Spam folder

These options can also be accessed by clicking the **Enter selection mode** button at the top-right of the Inbox. The Enter selection mode view also opens selection checkboxes next to each email.

At the top-left of the side bar, clicking the **Collapse** ▤ button will collapse the sidebar showing the email folders – the text labels will disappear leaving just the icons on show.

Directly above the Inbox is a search box. Click in it, enter your search term and then click the **magnifying glass** button to begin the search.

Composing, Formatting and Sending Email

Sending email messages with the Mail app is very straightforward. It may not provide some of the features and options found in more complex email clients such as Microsoft Outlook and Mozilla Thunderbird, but the ones it does provide are perfectly adequate as we will see.

Composing an Email Message

To write an email message, open the Mail app; it will open at the last received message. At the top-left of the screen, tap the **+ New mail** button. A new message window will open at the right as shown below:

1. In the To: field, type the address. As you type, matching contacts from the People app appear in a window – if the one you want is there, click it and it will be entered automatically

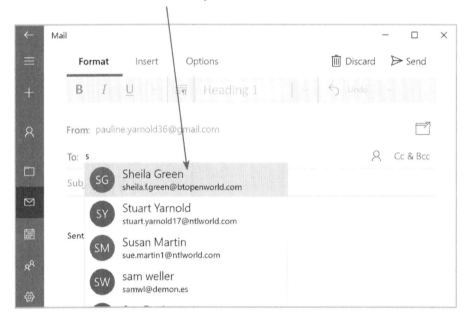

2. Click in the **Subject** field and then the type the subject (if there is one)

3. Click in the **Message** field (below the Subject field) and type your message. When you are ready to send it, click the **Send** button at the far-right of the toolbar

Formatting an Email Message

The Mail app in Windows 10 offers a good range of formatting options. These are all available from the Formatting toolbar that automatically opens when you open a new message window as we see below:

Formatting options include Bold, Italics and Underline. Click the down-arrow to the left of these to open a menu of font-related options.

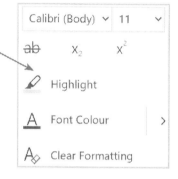

From the drop-down menu at the top, you can select from a huge range of fonts and font sizes. You can apply coloured highlighting to selected sections of text with the Highlight tool, while the Font colour tool lets you change the colour of the text.

Next to the Font options button is the Paragraph formatting button.

Options provided here include bullets – type, shape and size, numbering – a range of numbering layouts, indents, text alignment and justification, line spacing and paragraph spacing.

Finally, you can select from a list of different Headings by clicking the down-arrow to the right of Heading 1 or Heading 2.

This includes headings of different fonts, font sizes, different colours and italicized headings.

Attaching Files To Your Messages

Sometimes you will want to attach something to an email – this can be a picture, a document or a link. The Mail app has this covered as well:

On the Formatting toolbar, click the **Insert** tab to reveal the following options:

Files – clicking the **Files** button opens the Documents folder in File Explorer – if the document you want to send is here, just click it and it will be attached to the email. If not, use File Explorer to browse to where it is located.

Table – clicking **Table** inserts a table into the body of the email. You will now see different, table-related, options on the toolbar.

Pictures – clicking **Pictures** opens the Pictures folder. Click the required picture and it will be inserted into the body of the email. Different options will now be available on the toolbar – these will let you rotate, crop and resize the picture as necessary.

Link – if you wish to send a link to a web page in an email, click the **Link** option. This will open a box into which you can enter the address of the link and also a name for it.

Options

The third tab on the formatting toolbar is **Options**. This lets you specify an importance level for the email – either High or Low. You can also set the language of the text used in the email from the language drop-down box. If, like the author, your spelling ability is not as good as it could be, click **Spelling** to run a spell check on what you have written.

Create a Signature

By default, every email you send from the Mail app will be signed 'Sent from Mail for Windows 10'. Change this as follows:

1. At the bottom-right of the email folders sidebar, you will see a Settings button. Click this and then click **Signature**

2. Under Signature, either switch it off or enter your own in the signature box below

Create Contacts With the People App

All computing devices these days provide an address book in which you can store contact details of the people in your life. The version offered by Window 10 is the People app.

The People and Mail apps are inextricably linked – start typing an address into an email and Mail will immediately query the People app to see if it is holding an address for it. If so, it will appear in a window from where you can select it.

However, for this to work, the address must be in the People app in the first place. Lets see how to do this.

Create a Contact
The People app is very simple and creating an entry couldn't be easier:

1. At the bottom of Mail's sidebar, click the **Switch to People** button

2. The Contacts screen opens – click the **+** button

3. A new contact window opens – enter the contact's details in the fields provided

4. If a required field isn't available, scroll down and click **+ Other** to open a list of more fields from which you can choose

5. If you have a photo of the contact, click **Add photo** at the top-left of the window – this opens the Photos app. Find the picture, select it and resize it as necessary. Then click the **Apply** button at the top-right

cont'd

Import a List of Contacts

If you already have a list of contacts created with a different email program, you can import them to the People app and save yourself the bother of entering them manually as described on the previous page. Having done so, you can then access the People app from Mail with a single click.

1. Open the People app, either from Mail or the Start menu

2. The app opens and immediately searches the computer for email accounts You are then presented with a list of all the accounts it finds

3. You are given the option to import the contacts associated with these accounts

4. Click the account that you want to import contacts from

5. The contacts will now be imported to Mail as we see below

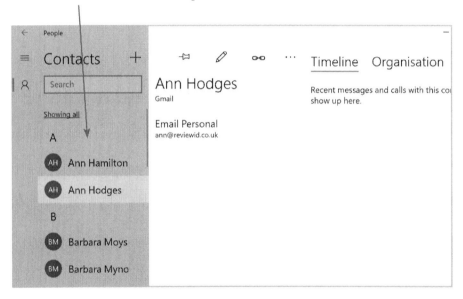

6. To access the contacts list, click the **Switch to People** button at the bottom of Mail's sidebar

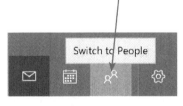

Organising Your Messages

Creating Folders

If you do a lot of emailing, it can be very helpful from an organisational perspective to place your messages in mailboxes that you have created for the purpose.

To do this with Mail:

1. Click **All folders** on the sidebar

2. Click the **+ Create new folder** button at the top-right of the new window

3. In the Name box that opens, give your mailbox a suitable name

4. Tap **Enter** on the keyboard to save it

Moving Messages

Having created some mailboxes, or if you are using the default ones provided with the Mail app, you can move messages to and from them as described below:

1. Open the folder (this can include the Inbox) that contains the message to be moved and right-click on it

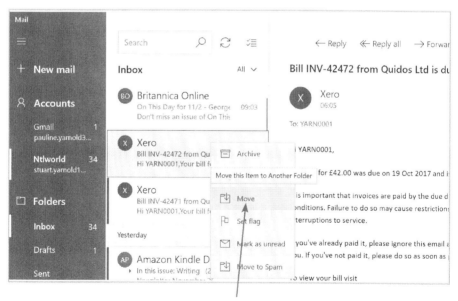

2. From the right-click menu, select **Move**

3. The account's mailbox list will open; just click on the one you want to move the message to and it's done.

cont'd

Favourite Folders

By default, the Mail app provides Inbox, Sent Mail and All Mail folders – these are shown in the folder list on the sidebar at the left. If you want access to any additional folders you have created for organisation purposes, you have to click the **More** option that's below to reveal the other folders.

Some of these folders may actually be more important than the default Mail folders and so you may want these to show up in the folder list as well.

To do this:

1. On the sidebar, click the **More** option to reveal your email folders

2. Locate the folder you want quick access to, right-click on it and choose **Add to Favourites**

The folder will be now available from the folder list and will be placed below the default Mail app folders.

You can also use this method to pin any of your email folders to the Windows 10 Start menu. When done, the pinned tile will show a count of new emails that are delivered to these folders.

CHAPTER 10
Working With Multimedia

Pictures and video are produced, transported and viewed as files, in a range of digital formats. With the appropriate software, your computer lets you view, edit, print and organise your photos and videos. This also applies to audio.

In Chapter 10, we demonstrate how to use your computer to get the best out of these activities. We also take a brief look at gaming with your Windows 10 PC.

Types of Image Format

There are a wide range of digital image formats. While it isn't essential to know what these are, it can be helpful on occasion. The main formats are:

BMP (Windows bitmap)

This format handles graphics files within Windows. The files are uncompressed, and therefore large, but they are widely accepted in Windows applications and so are simple to use.

GIF (Graphics Interchange Format)

This is format is limited to 256 colours. It is useful for graphics with relatively few colours such as diagrams, shapes, logos and cartoon style images. The GIF format supports animation. It also uses a lossless compression that is effective when large areas have a single colour, but ineffective for detailed images or dithered images.

JPEG (Joint Photographic Experts Group)

The JPEG/JFIF filename extension is JPG or JPEG, and it uses lossy compression. Nearly every digital camera can save images in the JPEG format, which supports 24-bit colour depth and produces relatively small files. JPEG files suffer degradation when repeatedly edited and saved.

PNG (Portable Network Graphic)

The PNG format was created as the successor to GIF. It supports trucolor and provides a lossless format that is best suited for editing pictures. Lossy formats like JPEG, on the other hand, are best for the final distribution of photographic images as they are usually smaller than PNG. PNG works well with web browsers.

Raw Image Format

The Raw Image format is used on some digital cameras to provide lossless or nearly-lossless compression. This produces much smaller file sizes than the TIFF formats (see below) from the same cameras.

Raw formats used by most cameras are not standardised or documented, and differ between camera manufacturers. Graphic programs and image editors may not accept some, or all, of them, so you should use the software supplied with the camera to convert the images for editing purposes and retain the raw files as originals and backup.

TIFF (Tagged Image File Format)

This is a flexible format that saves 24-bit and 48-bit colour, and uses the TIFF or TIF filename extension. TIFFs can be lossy and lossless, with some digital cameras using the LZW compression algorithm for lossless storage. TIFF is not well supported by browsers but is a photograph file standard for printing.

Windows 10's Photos App

Given how simple and basic it appears to be at first glance, the Photos app supplied with Windows 10 is a surprisingly powerful performer that is packed with features to help you view, edit and organise your digital images. It also lets you share your pictures via social networks and email.

The app has two main sections - Collection and Folders. In the Collection section, you'll see a collection of all your photos grouped by date taken and in reverse chronological order. If you want to quickly find photos from a certain time period without scrolling through all of the photos in your collection, click on a date to zoom out to a list of all previous months.

With regard to folders, the app will automatically create folders of photos based on the place they were shot, when they were shot and who is in them. Photos won't let you sort by people but you can create your own folders. Also, the app will 'pretty up' your folders by automatically choosing a cover image and starting off with a sample of the best or most popular pictures.

By default, the Photos app will automatically enhance photos – removing red eye and adjusting aspects such as brightness, contrast and colour. You can turn this off, however.

A potentially very useful feature is the automatic removal of duplicate pictures. If you have thousands of photos from different devices, it's quite likely that you have a number of duplicates from shuttling photos between those devices. This feature can save a lot of time when organising collections.

Windows 10 is designed to work on both computers and mobile devices, so syncing content and settings is a priority. Windows 10's Photos app achieves this through integration with OneDrive - see pages 64-66

Importing Pictures to the Photos App

The first step with the Photos app is getting some pictures into it. To do this:

1. Open the app from the Start menu and click the **Import** button

2. You'll then be asked where the pictures are - in a folder or on a device such as a camera, phone or USB drive. Select the option that applies

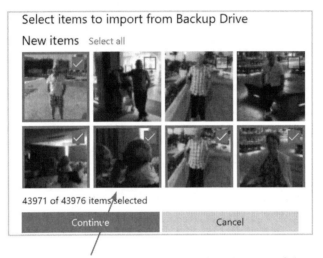

3. If any pictures are found, you'll be presented with a list of them. Each will have a check box that lets you deselect them if you so desire. When you have selected the ones you want to import, click **Continue** at the bottom

4. The next screen lets you specify where the pictures are to be stored. When you have done so, click the **Import** button. When the import is done, you'll see a confirmation message appear

Viewing Pictures in the Photos App

When viewing pictures with the Photos app, you can look at them in either the Collections view or the Folders view.

If you select the former, you are presented with a scrollable list of all your pictures, starting with the most recent. If you choose the latter, you get a list of folders, again, starting with the most recent. Click on a folder to open a list of the pictures it contains.

Having clicked on a picture to open it, at the top you will see a toolbar offering a number of options (click once on the picture to hide the toolbar).

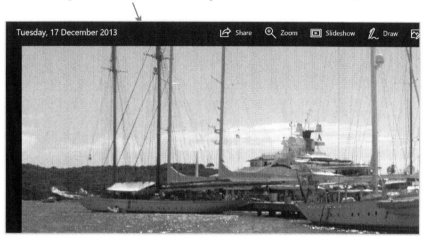

From left to right, these are:

- **Share** – this opens a list of apps with which the picture can be shared

- **Zoom** – Click this to get a close up view of the picture

- **Slideshow** – clicking Slideshow will start a full-screen slideshow

- **Enhance** – the Enhance button applies automatic image correction

- **Draw** – This gives you a number of pen options with which to draw on the picture

- **Edit** – clicking the Edit button opens a wide range of tools with which to edit the picture – we look at these on pages 142-143

- **Rotate** – this rotates the picture in 90 degree steps

- **See more** – this button provides more options. You can specify a different app for opening pictures of this type, you can copy it, you can print it and you can set it as wallpaper for both the Desktop and the Lock screen

Picture Editing Options

One of the great things about computers is the way they allow you to play about with pictures. You can blow them up, cut bits out of them, digitally enhance and alter them, and then use the finished result in any number of ways. This can be both for business and for fun. Whatever your reason for doing it, the Photos App provides you with the means.

Open the picture to be edited and click the **Edit** button on the toolbar. You will then see the editing tools appear on the right of the picture.

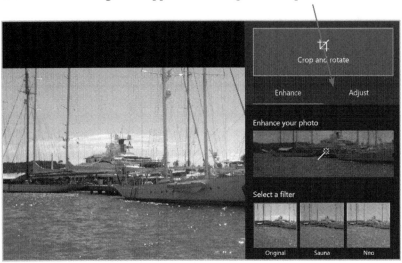

The first tool is **Crop and rotate** – this puts a handle at each corner with which you can 'crop' out parts of the picture. One example of how this can be used is to effectively zoom in on a particular feature in a picture.

Next are **Enhance** and **Adjust**. Both these options provide a number of editing tools that include:

The **Red eye** tool lets you remove the red eye effect where it is present. Move the circle over the affected eye and click to remove it. The **Retouch** tool can be used to remove small marks and blemishes by clicking on them.

The **Filters** tool gives you six built-in filters. These let you make instant changes to the look of a picture – black & white, for example.

Clicking **Light** opens four options on the right of the picture. These let you adjust the picture's light level, contrast, highlights and shadows. These adjustments can improve the look of a picture by a considerable degree.

Colour tools include Tint and Warmth. As with the Light tools, judicious use of these tools can take a so-so photo and make it look like it was taken by a pro. Overuse may have the opposite effect!

The **Vignette** tool creates a drop-shadow effect around the edges of the picture giving it an 'arty' feel, as we see in the image below:

As you make your edits, buttons on the toolbar below let you undo the edits, save the edited picture, and save the edited picture as a copy of the original.

Types of Video Format

As with pictures, there are many types of video format. For people who intend to work with video on their computer, it is well worth knowing the pros and cons of the most commonly used types. These are:

AVI (Audio Video Interleave

Developed by Microsoft, the AVI format is one of the oldest video formats. It is so universally accepted that many people consider it the de facto standard for storing videos on the computer. Due to it's simple architecture, AVI files are able to run on a number of different systems like Windows, Macintosh and Linux.

WMV (Windows Media Video)

Designed for web streaming applications, WMV files are the smallest video files used on the web as their file size decreases significantly after compression. This makes it an ideal format for uploading and sharing videos via social media sites such as FaceBook.

MOV (Apple QuickTime Movie)

Developed by Apple, the QuickTime file format is a popular type of video sharing and viewing format amongst Macintosh users, and is often used on the web and for saving video files. MOV files are not just limited to Apple computers – there is a free version of the QuickTime Player available for Windows. Considered one of the best looking file formats, MOV files are of high quality and are usually large.

FLV (Flash Video Format)

FLV files can be played with the Adobe Flash Player, web browser plug-ins and various third-party programs. Since virtually everyone has the player installed on their browser, it has become the most common online video viewing platform on the Internet today.

Almost all video sharing sites stream videos in Flash, so practically all browsers support, and are compatible with, the FLV format.

MPEG4 (Moving Pictures Expert group 4)

The MPEG4 video format uses separate compression for audio and video tracks – video is compressed with MPEG-4 or H.264 video encoding, while audio is compressed using AAC compression. File sizes are relatively small but the quality is high even after compression. The format is now becoming more popular than FLV for online video sharing as it compatible with both online and mobile browsers and is supported by HTML5.

Windows 10's Films & TV App

Window 10's Films & TV app brings the latest HD films and TV shows to your Windows 10 device.

It enables you to rent and buy new blockbuster films and favourite classics, or catch up on last night's TV. Films & TV also brings you instant-on HD and fast access to your video collection.

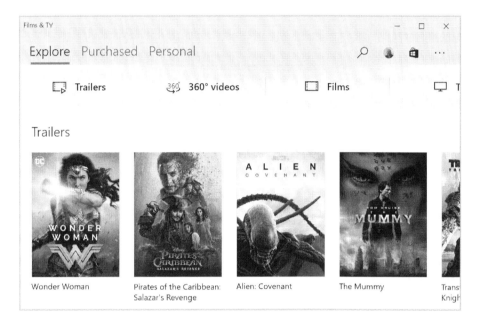

With it, you can:

• Rent and buy the latest films on your Windows 10 device

• Get the latest TV shows the day after they air

• Read customer and critic ratings when choosing programs

• Watch purchases and rentals on your Xbox, Windows 10 device, Windows Phone and on the Internet

• Find what you're looking for quickly and easily

• Get detailed descriptions of your favourite films and TV shows

• Use closed captioning – this is available for most films and TV shows

The Films & TV app plays most digital rights management (DRM)-free videos with the following file extensions: M4, MPEG4, MOV, ASF, AVI, WMV, M2TS, 3G2, 3GP2 and 3GPP.

Importing Video to the Films & TV App

When you first open the Films and TV app, it searches your computer for compatible videos. It doesn't look just in the default Windows video folder, which is C:\Users\Public\Videos, it looks everywhere. When it finds a folder that contains a video, it will continue to watch that folder in case more videos are added to it. To see what folders the app is monitoring:

1. Open the app from the Start menu

2. At the far-right of the toolbar, click the **More options** button and **Settings**

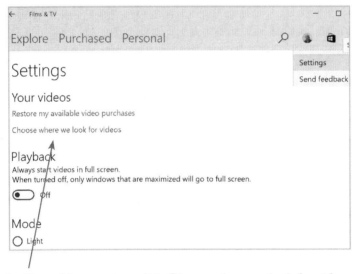

3. In the **Your videos** section, click **Choose where we look for videos**

4. The window that opens shows you the folders the app is watching

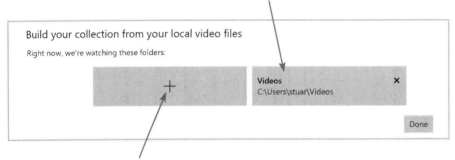

5. You can click the + button and designate a different folder, or more folders, to be monitored. You can remove the currently monitored folders by clicking the X button at the top-right

From this, you can see that videos aren't actually imported as such – the app's video list is simply a list of shortcuts to the videos.

Buying and Downloading Video

If you intend to watch films and TV on your computer, the Windows Store is one of the places you can get them from. Do it as follows:

1. On the app's toolbar, click the **Get films and TV in Store** button

2. The Windows Store will open at the **Films & TV** page

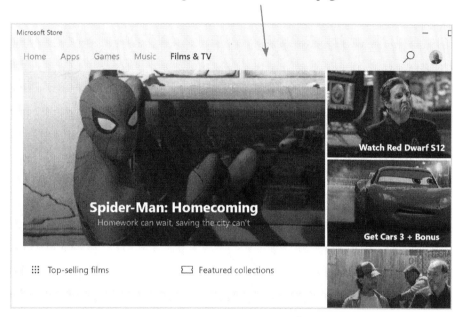

3. On the screen you will see top-selling films and TV programmes. As you scroll down the window, you'll see sections for new films, top film rentals, featured films, new TV programs, top-selling TV programs, featured TV programs and featured collections. Right at the bottom is a list of film genres

4. Click on an item to see detailed information about it. This usually includes a free trailer, a synopsis, the price and the cast and crew. There may also be reviews and ratings from people who have already watched it

5. When you're ready to buy, click the **Buy** or **Rent** button. A window will open offering options to either stream the movie or to download it to the computer to watch offline. Make your choice and click **Next**

6. The next window will ask you to enter your Microsoft password. Do so and click the **Sign in** button

7. Enter your payment details and the movie will then be downloaded or streamed

Playing a Film or Video

To play an item, be it a home video or a film downloaded from the Windows Store, open the Films & TV app.

1. On the toolbar, click **Purchased** or **Personal**. If you have any videos in the Videos folder (the only folder that the app watches initially), they will be listed in the window that opens. If you have videos in other folders that you want to add to the app, click the **Add Folders** box

2. The next window shows you the folders the app is watching (the Video folder) and invites you to add more by clicking the + button

3. Now browse your computer for folders to add to the app, clicking the **Add this folder to videos** button each time you find one. When you've finished, you will see all your video folders in one place

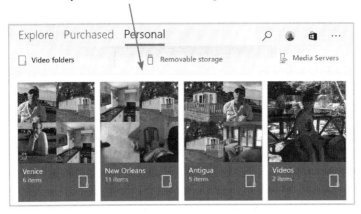

4   Find the film or video you want to play and click on it. The film opens in a new window with the playback controls at the bottom

148

Editing Video With Shotcut

The Films & TV app doesn't provide any options for editing video. So if you have a video that needs altering in some way, you need to go online and download a suitable program. One that we recommend is 'Shotcut', which can be downloaded from www.shotcut.org.

When you have installed it, open it from the Start menu. It will open as below:

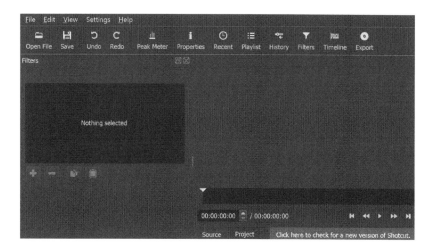

To open the video to be edited, click **Open File** on the toolbar and browse to where it is located. Click on it and it will open in Shotcut.

A number of editing options are provided on the toolbar. These include setting a new start or finish point, splitting the video, trimming out unwanted sections, plus adding a soundtrack, title, captions, animations and effects. You can also alter the brightness level, set the playback speed and compensate for shake.

cont'd

Trimming a Movie

To remove unwanted parts of a move with Shotcut, in the editing window drag the left-hand marker to where you want the movie to start.

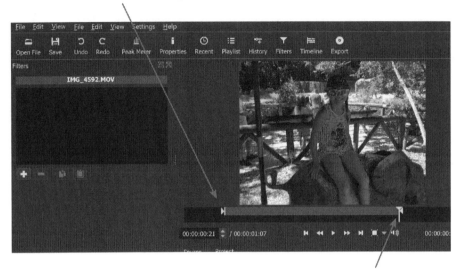

Now move the right-hand marker to where the movie is to end. Click **File** on the toolbar and click **Save**. Browse to where you want to save the video and then click **Save** again.

Editing a Movie

Shotcut provides a range of filters, which let you make many adjustments to both the look and sound of a video. These include brightness, colour, contrast, white balance, fade in and much more. To access these filters, click the Filters button on the toolbar. They open on the left.

How to Set Up Loudspeakers

Most desktop and laptop computers are equipped with audio facilities that are capable of producing high fidelity audio playback. On desktop machines, the sound card or motherboard will provide the connections for the various types of speaker setup. These range from simple stereo speakers to multiple speaker sets with surround sound. For a laptop or notebook, the options are often limited to microphone and headset sockets, though some laptops include more sophisticated connections such as the SPDIF (Sony Philips Digital Interface) used for home theatre connections.

You may have speakers attached to your computer or built into the casing of a portable computer. To check it out:

1. Open the Control Panel by typing **control** in the Taskbar search box and pressing **Enter**. In the Control Panel, click **Sound**

2. On the Playback tab, click **Speakers** and then **Configure**

3. Select your desired configuration, click **Next** and follow the prompts to finish and save the speaker configuration

Other options available from the Sound applet include configuring headphones (if connected), microphones (again, if connected) and changing the default sounds produced by Windows. The latter is located on the Sounds tab and includes options such as when an email is received and when a device is connected to the computer. Windows provides a range of sounds from which you can choose. You can also use sounds from other sources as well - just click the **Browse** button and then find and select the desired sound file.

The Groove Music Service

Groove is a Microsoft music service and has risen out of the ashes of Xbox Music. While the core of the service remains the same, with the launch of Windows 10, Groove has become available to millions around the world.

Groove Music is the app while Groove is the service. With a Groove music pass, you get access to Microsoft's catalogue of online music to stream or download for offline use. The pass is valid on Windows 10 as well as Windows Phone, iOS, Android, Xbox and the web, with prices per month varying per region. Signing up does require a Microsoft account, though if you're using Windows 10 you've probably already got one.

As with most other streaming services, your Groove music pass lets you subscribe to unlimited on-demand music from a huge catalogue. But, unlike the other services, Groove lacks a free, ad-supported listening option. If you don't want to pay for the subscription, however, you can still upload your music files to OneDrive to have them available for playing in Groove. You can also purchase songs and albums outright.

If you want to download music for offline listening, there are a couple of things to be aware of:

1. You can only have offline music on a total of five devices at any one time. So be sure to check your account (through the settings menu in Groove) and ensure any old devices have been deactivated. You can only remove one every 30 days

2. Whether you've got a collection of personal music from your own sources or amassed through online stores like iTunes and Google Play, the Groove app on Windows 10 will catalogue it and play it for you. In most cases, all you need to know is where on your computer the music is stored and tell the app where to find it

Groove doesn't just allow you to stream music from its online catalogue; you can also create your own personal cloud locker with OneDrive. By adding your music to OneDrive, you can get the Groove or Xbox Music apps to play it on all your devices.

Whether you have a Groove music pass or not, you may find yourself wanting to purchase tracks to listen to. This is now done through the Windows Store. You can either go directly to the Store app on your computer or tablet and press the Music tab, or access it through the Groove app.

Importing Music

Getting music into the Groove Music app is done as follows:

1. Open the app by clicking **Groove Music** in the Start menu. Then click the **Settings** button at the bottom of the sidebar

2. Under **Music on this PC**, click **Choose where we look for music**

3. In the new window, you'll see the folders that the app is using to build its music collection. As with the Films & TV app, these include the default Windows folders for files of this type

4. Click the **+** button to open File Explorer and browse to a folder containing music that you want to add to the app. Select it and then click the **Add this folder to Music** button. Repeat for any other folders you want to add

5. As you add more music to the folders being watched by Groove, it will be imported automatically

Viewing and Playing Your Music

Having got some music into the Groove app, you have three ways to view it: by album, by artist and by song – make your choice from the toolbar at the top. In the example below, we have chosen the Songs view and selected a song.

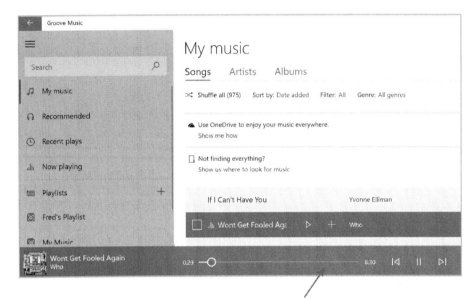

The playback controls are at the bottom of the screen and are the standard Previous, Play/Pause, Next, Shuffle, Repeat and Volume.

Playlists

A useful feature in the Groove app is Playlists. A playlist is a list of songs that can be played in sequential or shuffled order. Create one as follows:

1. Click the **+** button at the right of Playlists on the sidebar

2. A window will open in which you enter a name for the playlist. Click **Create playlist**

3. The playlist is created and added to the Playlist section on the sidebar

4. Go through your music collection and right-click on any song you want to add to the playlist – select **Add to** and then click the required playlist

To play the playlist, click on it in the sidebar.

We've explained how to get the music on your computer into the Groove app. Another option is buying and downloading music from the Windows Store. To do this, click the **There are tons of tracks to pick from** link under **Visit the Music Store** - the procedure for browsing and buying music is exactly the same as for films and TV programs.

CHAPTER 11

Keep Your Computer And Data Secure

The stuff on your computer – files, contacts, programs, email, etc, doesn't just appear there by magic – it is usually the result of years of using the device. Losing it all can be nothing short of a disaster as you are then faced with the task of creating it all again from scratch - if that's possible!

In this chapter, we focus on how to keep your computer, and the data on it, safe and secure.

Password-Protection Methods

We'll begin this chapter on the subject of passwords.

Standard Passwords

When you log on to your computer, you are asked for a password – this happens whether you are signing in with a Microsoft account or a local account – without one, you are not allowed into the computer.

Lets take a look at your options here:

1. On the Start menu, go to **Settings** > **Accounts**

2. Should you wish to change your current password, click **Sign-in options**. On the right, click **Change** under Password. A new screen opens in which you are asked for the current password. Enter it and click **Sign in**. In the next screen, enter the new password, click **Next** and then click **Finish**

3. Another option available to you is using a pin number instead of a password – many people find these easier to use. Under Pin, click the **Add** button. Enter your current account password and then click **Next**

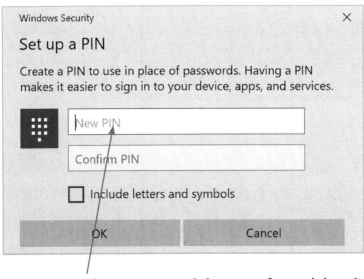

4. Enter the pin number, enter it again below to confirm, and then click **OK**. From now on, you sign in to your computer with the pin number

Picture Passwords

A more novel way of signing in to your computer is provided by the Picture password feature. This enables you to use a picture as a password. To 'authenticate' the picture, you have to perform three gestures on it:

1. In the Accounts sign-in options screen, click **Add** under Picture password

cont'd

2. In the window that opens, enter your Microsoft password and click **OK**

3. At the left, click **Select picture**

4. File Explorer opens – browse to the picture you want to use. Click **Use this picture**

5. In the next screen, draw three gestures on the picture – you can use any combination of circles, straight lines and taps

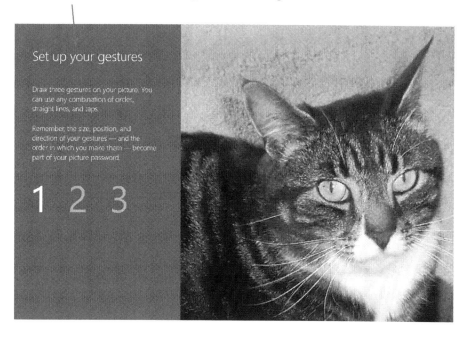

6. Repeat the gestures to confirm. Then click **Finish** and you're done

The next time you log on to the computer, you'll see the picture. Draw the three gestures and you're in.

Windows Hello Biometric Security System

Windows Hello is the name given to Microsoft's biometric security system for Windows 10. It employs facial- and fingerprint-recognition technology that scans your face or fingerprints when you sit down in front of the computer. If it recognises you, the computer is unlocked.

You can get going with Windows Hello in two ways:

- Purchase a laptop or tablet with the required security device built-in. This can be a special 'depth' camera or a fingerprint reader

- Add the security device to an existing setup

With regard to the cameras, they are not cheap so if you want to use the Hello feature, it may be better to buy a computer with one built in.

To set up Windows Hello on your computer:

1. On the Start Menu, go to Settings and click **Accounts**

2. Set up a pin number as explained on page 156 – this is required to use Windows Hello. That done, the Windows Hello settings will now be available

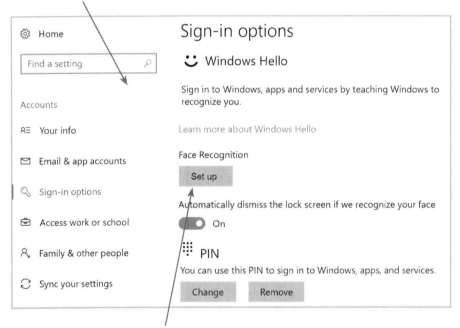

3. Click **Set up** under Face Recognition and then click **Get started**

4. From this point on follow the prompts. Note that these will vary according to the security device being used

The Pros and Cons of a Microsoft Account

When you first upgrade to Windows 10, you're encouraged to sign in with a Microsoft account. There are some benefits with this, as it allows any Windows 10 device you have to sync data and preferences for various Microsoft services such as OneDrive and the Windows Store. But this sharing feature also means surrendering quite a bit of personal information to Microsoft, which is something not everybody is comfortable doing.

For these people, the solution is what's known as a 'local account' which doesn't involve Microsoft in any way. None of your personal data is shared with the software giant but you do lose the advantages of account synchronisation.

You can set up a local account as follows:

1. Open the Start Menu and navigate to **Settings > Accounts > Your Account > Family and other people**

2. Under **Other people,** you'll see an option to **Add someone else to this PC**

3. Click this and then when you're prompted for an email address select **I don't have this person's sign-in information**

4. At the next screen, click **Add a user without a Microsoft account**

5. Enter the username and password you want for the account and click **Next**

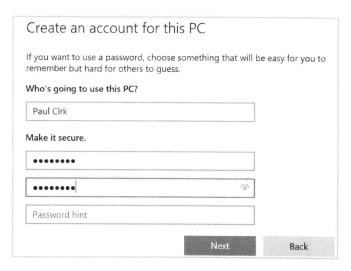

The new account is created and it will be a Standard one. However, you may want to upgrade it to an Administrator account. If so, when you're in the **Family & other people** section, click on the account, click **Change Account type** and then select **Administrator**. Whichever type you settle for, you will now be able to log-in to your computer without a Microsoft account.

How to Encrypt Your Data

Another password-related risk to the security of your data arises when your computer is stolen. The thieves may not be able to crack your password in order to gain access to the computer but they could simply take the hard drive out and install it in their own computer. The solution to this problem is data encryption and Windows 10 provides two utilities that you can use for this purpose. These are the Encrypting File System (EFS) and BitLocker Drive Encryption.

Encrypting File System (EFS)

This system encodes files and folders so they can only be read when you log-on to the computer with the associated user account. During the encoding process, an encryption key is created and stored within the user account. If an attempt is made to access the file from a different user account, the encryption key won't be available and so the file in question cannot be decrypted. To do it:

1. Open File Explorer and browse to the folder that contains the file

2. Right-click on the folder and click **Properties**

3. Click the **Advanced** button

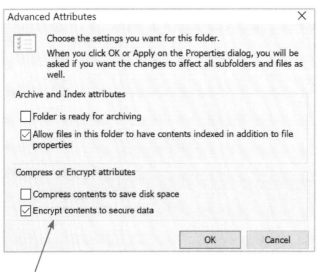

4. In the Advanced Atributes dialogue box, check **Encrypt contents to secure data** and click **OK**

5. On the General tab, click **Apply** and, in the Confirm Attribute Changes window, click **OK**

6. Click **OK** once more and the encryption procedure begins – you will see a progress indicator

When the encryption is complete, check the folder in File Explorer. You will notice that its name text has now changed to green – this is the only indication that a folder has been encrypted. Another user logging in to your computer via a different account will be able to see and open the folder but will not be able to open the files inside it.

Please note that the Encrypting File System is only available on the Professional and Enterprise editions of Windows 10. If you are using the Home edition, the encryption feature will be grayed out and unavailable.

BitLocker Drive Encryption

EFS is fine for encrypting folders and individual files. However, you can also choose to encrypt an entire drive. If so, you need Windows BitLocker feature. As with the Encrypting File System, BitLocker is only available on the Pro and Enterprise editions of Windows 10.

If you have either of these, you can use Bitlocker as follows:

1. Type **bitlocker** into the Taskbar search box and press **Enter**

2. The **BitLocker Drive Encryption** window opens

3. All the drives on your computer are displayed. Click on the one you want to encrypt

4. After initialising, a window will open asking you to enter a password with which to unlock the drive. Do so and click **Next**

5. At the next window, specify where the recovery key is to be saved and then click **Next**

6. You will now be asked if you want to encrypt the entire drive or just the part of it that's currently in use. Make your choice and click **Next**. Then in the next window, click **Start encrypting**

When a drive has been encrypted with Bitlocker, all data subsequently added to it is automatically encrypted as well.

Save Important Data Online

We've mentioned OneDrive a few times in this book and seen how it can be used to access and share your files from anywhere. Another way it can be used is to make sure important data is automatically saved online so if anything happens to your computer, a copy will always be available. Do it as follows:

1. Open File Explorer and browse to the folder containing the data to be syncronised

2. Left-click on the folder and drag it across to the OneDrive folder on the sidebar and release it

3. Now access your OneDrive at **www.OneDrive.live.com**

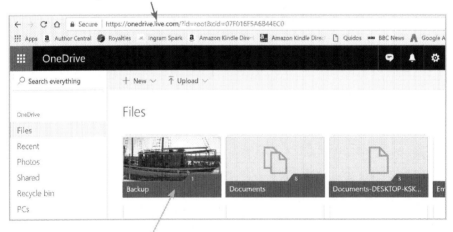

4. You will see that your folder is safely stored online. You can now use the folder on your PC as a backup folder – any data you add to it will automatically be copied to the online folder in OneDrive

Back Up Your Files Automatically

There are a number of issues that can be experienced when working with files. You may simply have lost one. Or, you may have deleted one by accident. A file can become corrupted and refuse to open. All these, and more, can be resolved with the Windows 10 File History utility. Before you can use it though, you need to get a separate drive on which to store the backup. Once you have:

1. Open the Start menu and click **Settings**

2. In Settings, click **Update & Security** and then **Backup**

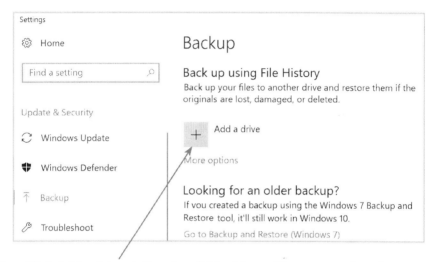

3. Click **Add a drive**. A list of available drives will appear – select the one you want to use for the backup

4. Click the **Automatically back up my files** option to **On**

5. Click **More options** and in the new window, click **Back up now**

6. Before you exit this window, scroll down to the **Back up these folders** section. The folders listed are the ones that are backed up – make sure everything you want to back up is in one of these folders. If not, click the **Add a folder** button, browse to the required folder, select it and click the **Choose this folder** button

From this point on, File History will work silently in the background backing up the specified folders to the backup drive. By default, the backup is updated every hour, which is something you can change if you want to by opening the Backup options screen and selecting a different period. You can also specify how long Windows is to keep the backup - the default is forever but you can set it to be between one month and two years.

See pages 173-174 for how to restore files from the File History utility.

Create a Complete System Backup

The File History utility is fine as far as it goes but it does not let you create a complete backup of your system. For this, you need to use another of Window 10's utilities - Back up and Restore.

1. Open the Control Panel

2. Click **Back up and Restore (Windows 7)**

3. At the left of the screen, click **Create a system image**

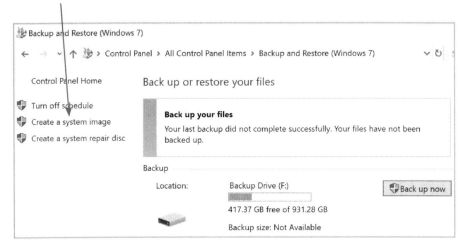

4. Windows will look for a separate drive on which to place the system image backup. You can also save it on DVD discs or to a network location. Make your choice and click **Next**

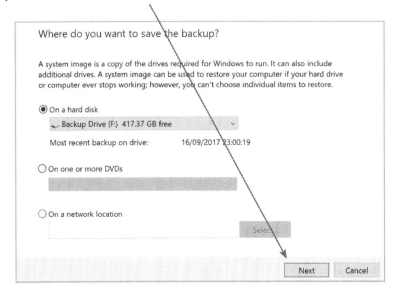

cont'd

5. At the next screen, select all the drives (assuming you have more than one) to be included in the backup

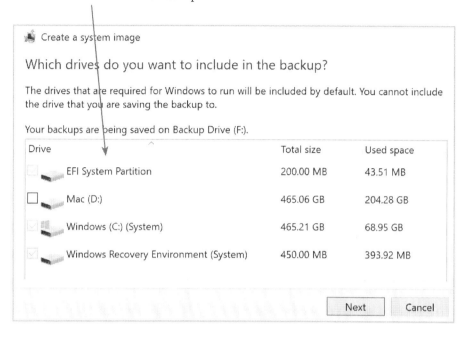

6. Click **Next** and then **Start backup** at the final screen

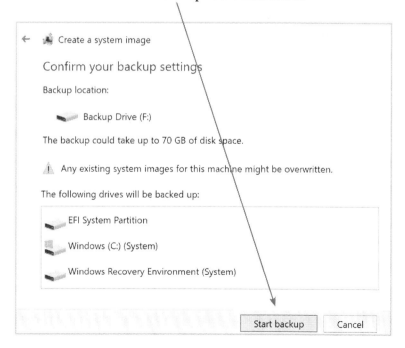

Restoring From a System Backup

When your system image backup has been built (and this can take several hours), you then need to create a system repair disc which you use with the system image to restore your computer. To do this:

1. Open Back up and Restore (Windows 7) as previously described

2. At the left of the screen, click **Create a system repair disc**

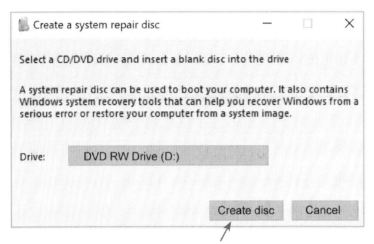

3. Make sure there is a disc in the CD/DVD drive and then click **Create disc.** The procedure takes just a few minutes

Should you ever have reason to restore your computer from the system image backup, do the following:

1. Place the system repair disc in your DVD drive

2. Restart the computer

3. When prompted, press any key to boot the computer from the disc

4. From the recovery options displayed, select **System Image Recovery**

The computer will now be restored from the system image to how it was when the image was created – any data created since will be lost.

If you don't have a CD or DVD drive in your computer, you can create a recovery drive with a USB flash drive instead. Open the Control Panel and click **Recovery**. At the top of the window, click **Create a recovery drive** and follow the instructions. The recovery drive works in much the same way as the system repair disc – connect it to the computer, restart the computer, find the **System Image Recovery** option and go from there.

Antivirus Software

Antivirus programs are designed to prevent, search for, detect and remove software viruses, and other malicious software like worms, trojans and adware.

Windows 10 provides a built-in antivirus program called Windows Defender. Access its settings by typing **windows defender** in the Taskbar search box and pressing **Enter**. The program is a fairly basic example of its type and is on by default. Note that there is no way to turn it off.

However, if you install a third-party antivirus program, Windows Defender will be automatically disabled and then re-enabled should you subsequently uninstall the third-party program.

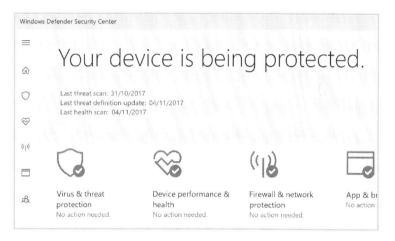

For all that it's straightforward, Windows Defender does have advantages. It's built-in, won't harass you with pop-ups and is simpler than some competing antivirus programs. Also, it won't attempt to harvest your browsing data as some free antivirus programs have started doing in an attempt to make a profit. Plus, it's free!

Overall, Windows Defender provides reasonably good protection and will probably be fine for most computers, along with some common sense and good security practices. However, if you're regularly downloading pirated applications and engaging in other high-risk behavior, you may want to disable Windows Defender and get something that offers a higher level of protection.

We also suggest an anti-exploit program to protect your web browser and plug-ins, which are the most targeted by attackers. One that we recommend is **MalwareBytes Anti-Exploit**. Get it at www.malwarebytes.com.

If you are looking for something better than Windows Defender, the ones to go for are **Kaspersky AntiVirus** and **BitDefender**. Both are consistently ranked at the top of the detection rate charts.

Privacy Issues in Windows 10

Personal privacy is a serious concern for anyone who surfs, shops or banks online. Google, Facebook, advertisers, hackers and others are all constantly trying to get your information so they can make money out of you.

This includes Microsoft. With every version of Windows, it's digging further and further into your personal life and Windows 10 is no exception. In fact, it introduces some new features that collect your data like never before. And by default, they are all turned on. Fortunately, you can turn them off if you know where to look.

The main offenders are:

Advertising
Like every other major online company, Microsoft is using targeted advertising to increase revenue. That means it's sending advertisers your data so they know what advertisments to send you. While you can't shut off the advertising, you can stop advertisers from seeing what you're doing.

Do this by going to **Start** > **Settings** and selecting **Privacy**. In Privacy, go to General and make sure **Let apps use advertising ID ...** is switched to **Off**. This stops advertisers getting your advertiser ID when you visit a page.

Location
Still on the Privacy screen, click **Location**. Here, you can tell Windows to stop tracking your location entirely, or specify which apps can and can't use your location. Location is useful for apps like the Weather app or when you're looking at maps because you don't have to put in your address every time.

The downside is that other apps might use it to keep tabs on you.

Cortana
As we have seen, Cortana is Microsoft's digital personal assistant. In order to provide you with information when requested, it has to learn as much about you as possible and it does this by monitoring your movements, browsing habits, contacts, calendar and more. If you don't think you'll use Cortana, you can turn it off by clicking in the Taskbar search box and clicking the **Notebook** icon at the left. Then click **Settings** and turn off the various Cortana options.

CHAPTER 12

Troubleshooting & Maintenance

Your computer is a machine and, like all machines, it will go wrong from time to time. Windows provides a number of tools that can help you diagnose and repair most problems, and in this chapter we show you what they are and how to use them.

A related issue is maintenance. If you don't keep your computer properly maintained, its performance will be adversely affected. Read on to find out how to keep it running smoothly.

Isolating the Problem

Troubleshooting, whatever is being investigated, can be approached in various ways. With computers, probably the most common is the 'flailing around' method. This is where the user, who almost certainly has little or no knowledge of what goes inside their computer's casing, starts frantically clicking this, that and the other in the desperate hope that, somehow, it just might do the trick.

Unfortunately, it almost never does. An approach that is far more likely to produce results is the considered approach in which you actually think about what has just happened (or not happened, as the case may be). In almost all cases, this will enable you to narrow down the potential causes of the problem and thus vastly increase the chances of actually finding it.

Things to consider include:

- **Error messages** – it is an unfortunate fact that the majority of computer error messages are either just phrased rather badly or are totally incomprehensible. Many of them do, however, contain error codes that can be useful as in the example below

We couldn't activate Windows

Error contacting Microsoft. Please make sure your device is connected to the Internet.

Error Code:0x8007267c

Close

Try doing an Internet search for the code and see what comes up – usually other people somewhere in the world have experienced the same problem and you may get the solution this way. Or, you can quote the code to a support technician

- **Windows settings** – Windows is chockful of things you can click. Think back – did you recently change anything? If you did and the problem showed up afterwards, you immediately have a good line of attack. If you can remember what it was that you changed, reverse that change and see what happens

- **Program settings** – computer faults are not restricted to Windows – the programs on it are just as likely to give trouble. If you recently changed something on a program that is now misbehaving, reverse the change. If the problem is still there, check to see if an update is available for the program

- **New software** – installing software on your computer is a common way of screwing it up. Most programs are fine but there are plenty of others out there that are anything but. The best move you can make whenever you are experiencing issues is to restart the computer – this action resets internal settings and can resolve a whole host of issues.

  If the problem is still present, use the computer for a while without running the program – if the problem goes away, you know what's causing it. Before giving up on the program and uninstalling it, make sure the version you have installed is compatible with Windows 10 – if not look for an updated version. If all else fails though, you will have to uninstall the program.

- **Software update** – downloading and installing updates to existing programs can also be the cause of issues. Unlikely as it may seem, this advice also apples to Windows itself. Windows 10 downloads and installs updates automatically (although you can put a stop to this in the settings).

  If a problem suddenly springs up immediately after a software update, the update has to be suspect. Check it out in the Control Panel by opening the Programs and Features utility. On the sidebar at the left, click **View installed updates**. You will now see all the updates and the dates they were installed. To uninstall one, right-click on it and click **Uninstall**

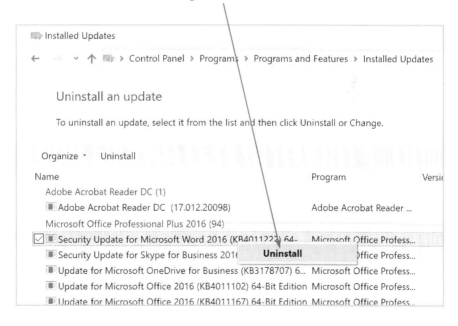

- **Device drivers** – installing hardware devices on your computer can cause problems if the device's driver is incompatible. This particular issue is easily resolved with the Windows System Restore utility – see page 175

Initial Troubleshooting Steps

If you follow the advice just given, you will usually be able to narrow the fault down to its approximate location. Feeling pleased with yourself, you may now be tempted to dive in and fix it.

However, before you get carried away, there are a number of very simple steps you can take that may well resolve the issue without you having to get your hands dirty.

- **Shut everything down** – by this, we don't mean Windows – just close all running applications. Every application that is open is using system resources such as memory and processor cycles.

  Shutting these programs down releases the resources and can have a dramatic effect on the computer. To do this, open the Task Manager (right-click on the Start button and click **Task Manager**). You will see a list of the programs currently running. Just right-click on them and then on the menu that opens, click **End task**.

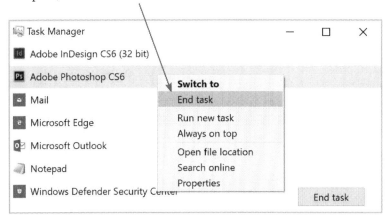

- **Restart the computer** – turning the computer off for a minute or so and then starting it up again is a well-known method of resolving hardware conflicts. The short period the computer is off gives the devices time to shut down properly

- **Connections** – a surprising amount of computer problems aren't really problems at all – it's just that the user has forgotten to flick the switch that turns a device on. On a similar vein, incorrect, missing or flaky connections are also common – check the cable is securely connected and connected to the right device

- **Troubleshooters** – Windows 10 provides a number of automated troubleshooters that can check (and also resolve) various types of problem. We take a closer look at these on page 176

Restoring Your Files

On page 163, we explained how the File History utility can be used to create backups of your files. Here, we explain how to use it to restore a missing or damaged file.

1. Use File Explorer to navigate to the folder where you need to recover a file

2. Right-click on the folder and then click **Restore previous versions**

3. In the new window click the **Previous Versions** tab

4. You will now see a list of all the versions of the folder held by File History

5. Select the one you want to restore from

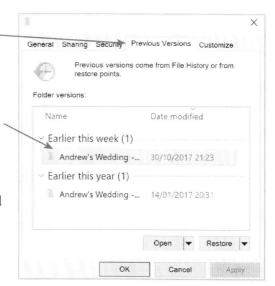

You'll then be presented with two options. The first is **Open**, which lets you restore individual files from the folder.

The second is **Restore**, which restores the entire folder and all it's contents.

cont'd

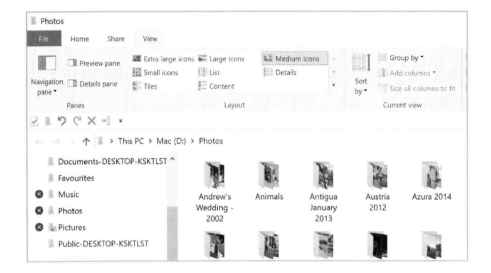

6. If you select the first option, **Open**, and the file you want is in a subfolder as in the example above, click on it and, if necessary, the one after that until you have drilled down to the file to be restored

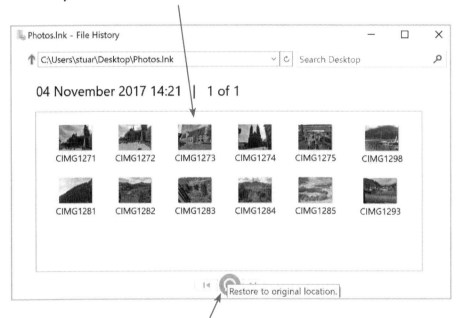

7. When you have found the file, select it and then click the **Restore to original location** button at the bottom of the window. If you want to restore all the files in the folder, select them all before clicking the Restore button

Undo System Changes With System Restore

What is System Restore?

System Restore is a Windows feature that lets you revert your computer's state (including system files, installed applications, Windows Registry and system settings) to that of a previous point in time. This lets you recover from system malfunctions or other serious problems.

For example, the installation of a program or a driver can cause an unexpected change to your computer or cause Windows to behave unpredictably. Usually, uninstalling the program or driver corrects the problem. If uninstalling doesn't fix the problem however, you can try restoring your computer's system to an earlier date when everything worked correctly.

System Restore uses a feature called system protection to regularly create and save restore points on your computer. These restore points contain information about registry settings and other system information that Windows uses. You can also create restore points manually.

Enabling System Restore

To enable System Restore:

- Type **system restore** into the Taskbar search box and press **Enter**

- The System Properties window opens at the System Protection tab. Under Protection Settings, click **Configure**

- Tick the **Turn on system protection** radio button and click **OK**

System Restore will now automatically create restore points whenever potentially damaging changes are made to the system. These can then be used to 'undo' these changes if necessary.

To create a restore point manually, open the System Properties window as described above and click the **Create** button.

Using System Restore

Open the System Properties window as already explained . Under the System Protection tab, click the **System Restore** button. You will now see a list of all the restore points that have been made. Choose one made prior to the fault manifesting itself, click **Next** and then click **Finish**. When the restore procedure is complete, the computer will reboot back into Windows. System Restore can also be used from a system repair disc and a recovery drive.

Note that System Restore isn't intended for backing up personal files, so it cannot help you recover a personal file that has been deleted or damaged. Use the File History utility for this purpose.

Windows Troubleshooters

Windows provides a number of troubleshooters that can help to diagnose problems. In some cases, they can even fix the problem.

To access the troubleshooters:

1. Open the Control Panel

2. Click **Troubleshooting**

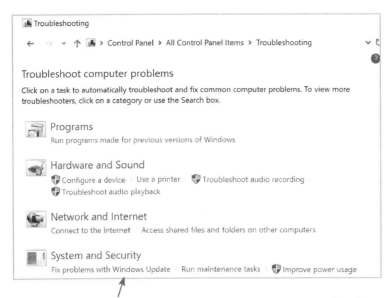

3. You will see four categories of troubleshooters – Programs, Hardware and Sound, Network and Internet, and System and Security. Each has a sub-category below in blue

4. Open the one most closely related to your problem. You will now see a list of troubleshooters for the selected category. Click the one you want to try

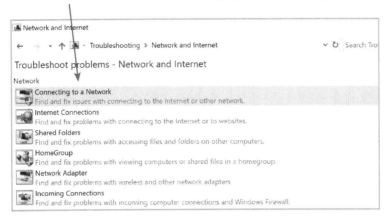

cont'd

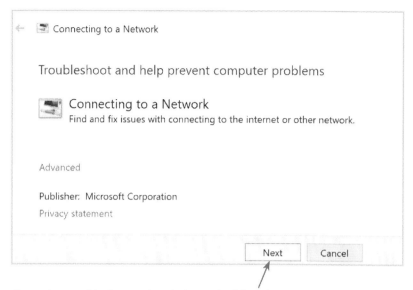

5. Start the troubleshooter by clicking the **Next** button at the bottom of the window

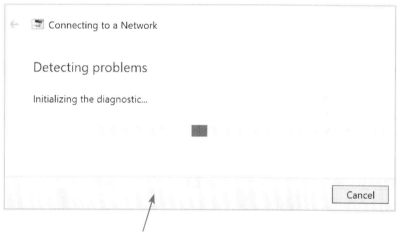

6. The troubleshooter attempts to find the cause of the problem. From this point on a number of different scenarios can occur depending on what the troubleshooter finds and the type of problem. Just follow the prompts.

Using the Windows Recovery Environment

What is it?
On page 166, we describe how to make a system repair disc and a recovery drive. These are necessary in order to restore a computer from a system image backup. When used, they boot the computer into what's known as the Windows Recovery Environment.

The RE is essentially a simplified, scaled-back version of Windows and is used to boot the system when it cannot boot normally or run in a stable manner. Within the recovery environment, a number of recovery tools are available that can be used to diagnose and repair problems with Windows. For example, automatic repair and troubleshooting tools that can test disk and file integrity. They are often able to fix common disk problems and restore files damaged by disk failures, malware activity or user errors.

Accessing the Windows Recovery Environment
There are a number of ways to access the RE and the avenue you take is largely dependent on the problem you are experiencing. If you can still get into Windows, you can do it from Update & Security.

1. Open the Start menu and click **Settings**

2. Click **Update & Security** and then click **Recovery**

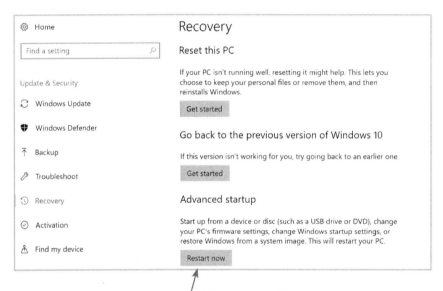

3. Under Advanced start-up, click **Restart now**. The computer will now reboot into the recovery environment

If, however, you cannot get into Windows you need to access the recovery environment as described on page 180.

Windows 10's Reset Utility

In a situation whereby you are experiencing minor issues with your computer that do not warrant the rigmarole of restoring from a backup, Windows provides a tool that may be just the thing you need.

This is the Reset utility. Reset gives you a quick and easy way to start with a clean slate while, at the same, time maintaining your apps, data, Windows settings and user profiles. Reset automatically sets all this stuff aside then puts it back where it belongs once the operating system is reinstalled. The result is a clean slate for Windows but with your configuration settings and data intact.

To reset your computer:

1. Open the Start menu and click **Settings**

2. Click **Update & Security**

3. Click **Recovery**

4. Under Reset this PC, click **Get started**

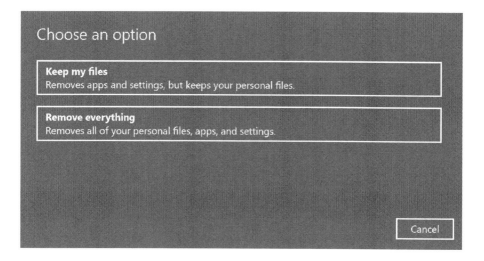

5. You are presented with two options: **Keep my files** and **Remove everything**. Select the first option and click **Reset** in the next screen

The computer will now reboot to the Desktop. Note that the Keep my files option will not restore the software you have installed. It will restore Windows 10 apps but not third-party software. This is to avoid re-installing software that might be the cause of the problem.

When the reset procedure is finished, a file listing any applications that were not installed is placed on the Desktop so you know what software is missing.

cont'd

The second option offered by Reset is **Remove everything.** This removes everything – files, apps and settings, and returns your computer to how it was when brand new.

For situations where you cannot get into Windows to access the Reset utility, you will have to to use the Windows Recovery Environment and either a system repair disc or a USB recovery drive as described on page 166.

Assuming a USB recovery drive is being used, the procedure is:

1. Connect the USB drive to a USB port on the computer

2. Start the computer

3. Windows will automatically boot from the recovery drive and present you with a number of troubleshooting and repair options

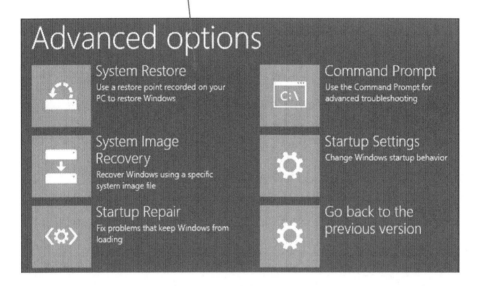

4. Select the most appropriate option and go from there

Remove Redundant Files With Disk Cleanup

Disk Cleanup is a Microsoft software utility first introduced with Windows 98 and included in all subsequent releases of Windows. It allows users to remove files that are no longer needed or that can be safely deleted - especially files the presence of which may not be obvious to you, such as temporary files used by Windows or when browsing the Internet.

Use it as follows:

1. Type **disk cleanup** into the Taskbar search box and press **Enter**. The utility opens

2. If you have more than one drive in your system, select the one to be cleaned up from the drop-down box

3. The utility will now calculate how much space can be reclaimed

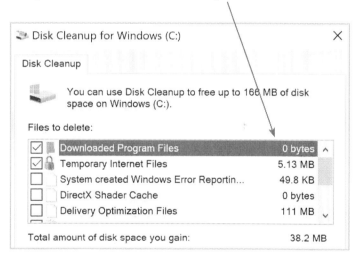

4. You will also see the location of the files to be deleted. You can deselect any of these by unchecking the box at the left

5. Click **OK** and the selected files will be removed from the computer

Optimise Hard Drive Performance

Defragmenting your hard drive is an integral part of keeping your PC healthy and, to this end, Windows provides the Optimise Drives defragmentation utility. It is very simple to use and can give a considerable boost to your computer's performance.

For the uninitiated, fragmentation is a phenomenon that causes drive storage space to be used inefficiently, reducing capacity or performance, and often both. Removable storage devices such as USB flash drives can also become fragmented.

The Optimise Drives utility rearranges fragmented data so your disks and drives can work more efficiently. By default, it is set to run automatically every week but you can also do it manually.

Open and run the utility as follows:

1. Type **defragment** into the Taskbar search box and press **Enter**

2. The Optimize Drives utility will open

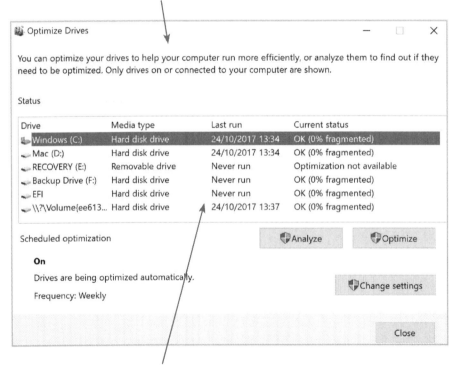

3. You will see all the drives in your system, their current defragmentation status, and the date they were last defragmented

4. Select a drive and click **Analyse** to see if it requires optimising

5. If it does, click the **Optimise** button to start the process. Note that this can take a long time depending on the amount of fragmentation and the size of the drive

In the Scheduled optimisation section, you'll see a **Change settings** button. This lets you set up an optimisation schedule on selected drives. To do this:

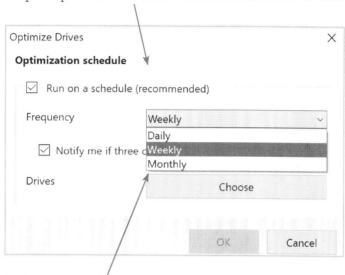

1. Set the frequency of the optimisation – options are Daily, Weekly and Monthly. Make your choice and then click the **Choose** button

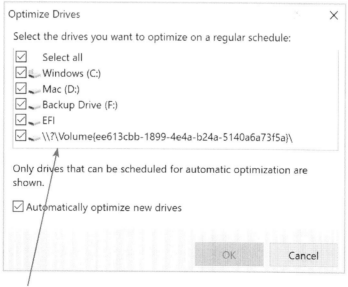

2. Select the drives to include in the schedule and then click **OK**

Optimise Windows 10's Performance

More performance enhancement tools can be found by going to the Control Panel and clicking **System**. In the System window, click **Advanced system settings** at the left. Then click the **Settings** button in the Performance section to open the Performance Options utility.

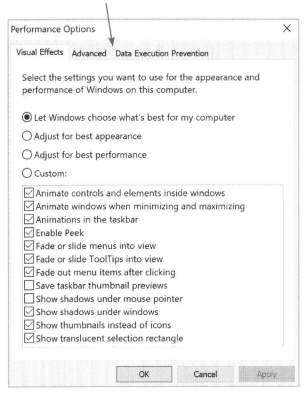

At the top are four options and in the section below are all the visual effects used on the computer. These all make a hit on its performance so disabling any that you don't need will give you a slight boost in speed.

The **Let Windows choose what's best for my computer** option will turn on most of the visual effects. **Adjust for best appearance** turns on all the effects, while **Adjust for best performance** turns them all off. The final option, **Custom**, lets you choose which effects to turn on.

Click the **Advanced** tab and you will see options for allocating processor resources and virtual memory. With regard to the processor, you can set it for the best performance of Programs or of Background services.

Virtual memory is a paging area that Windows creates on the computer's drive and uses as extra memory. If you know what you are doing, you can adjust the size of this file; if you don't, we recommend you leave well alone.

Make Old Programs Work With Windows

As Windows 10 is a relatively recent operating system, some programs designed for use with the older technologies found in previous editions struggle with it. This is a well known issue and is called program incompatibility.

Compatibility Modes

To overcome this problem, Windows provides a Compatibility modes feature that basically tricks programs into thinking they're running on the version of Windows they were designed for. Many older Windows programs will run fine when using this mode, when otherwise they wouldn't.

Windows 10 should automatically enable compatibility options if it detects an application that needs them, but you can enable these yourself:

1. Open the program's folder and locate its executable file (.exe)

2. Right-click on the .exe file and click **Properties** at the bottom

3. Open the Compatibility tab

4. Run the compatibility troubleshooter. This gives you two options: try recommended settings or to troubleshoot the program by choosing compatibility settings based on the problems you're having with it

5. If neither option does the trick, check the **Run this program in compatibility mode for** checkbox and, from the drop-down box, select the required edition of Windows.

6. Click **Apply** and then **OK**

If the program still doesn't run properly, either get an updated version (if one's available) or thank it for all its hard work and retire it.

Get Information About Your System

Troubleshooting a computer often requires detailed information about the computer in question or a part of it. Windows gives you two types of information – basic and detailed:

Basic

For a brief summary of the main elements in your system, open the Control Panel and click **System**:

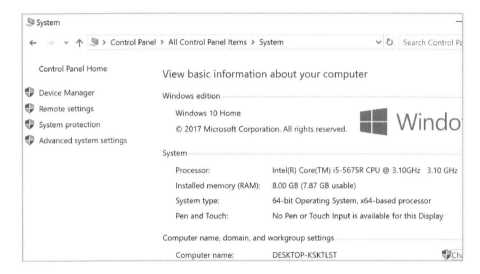

Detailed

For detailed information about your system, type **system information** into the Taskbar search box and press **Enter**:

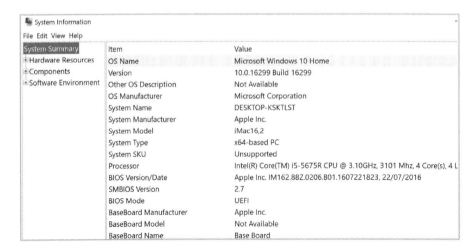

Index

X

Y

Z

———

Printed in Great Britain
by Amazon